FACTORY-ORIGINAL
FORD CAPRI MK II & MK III

The Originality Guide to all Capri models 1974-1987

BY JAMES TAYLOR
PHOTOGRAPHY BY SIMON CLAY

Herridge & Sons

Published in 2018 by
Herridge & Sons Ltd
Lower Forda, Shebbear
Beaworthy, Devon EX21 5SY

© Copyright James Taylor 2018

Design: Muse Fine Art & Design

All rights reserved. No part of this publication may be reproduced in any form or by any means without the prior written permission of the publisher and the copyright holder.

ISBN 978-1-906133-81-8
Printed in China

CONTENTS

ACKNOWLEDGEMENTS 6

FORD CAPRI MK II, 1974-1978 8

CAPRI MK II DETAILS 16

FORD CAPRI MK III, 1978-1986 52

CAPRI MK III DETAILS 60

THE AFTERMARKET SPECIALS 106

APPENDIX A: IDENTIFICATION 116

APPENDIX B: GLASS DATING 124

ACKNOWLEDGEMENTS

The original plan when writing this book was to produce a single book covering all three varieties of the Ford Capri. It soon became apparent that this plan would never work because there was just too much information for one volume. So *Factory-Original Ford Capri Mk1* appeared as a separate volume in 2017, and it made sense to keep the Mk II and Mk III cars together here because they have quite a lot in common.

This page gives me the opportunity to say thank you to everybody who helped out in the preparation of this book. I relied heavily on the knowledge and advice of Kevin Hickling for the Mk II pages, and for the Mk III section I relied on Francis Ellingworth. Both of them are very busy people and I probably tried their patience to the limit, but they know and I know that their input made this book much better than it would otherwise have been. I also grabbed a huge amount of information from a huge number of web sources – and discarded a lot of it as inaccurate or pure invention. Treat this as a warning! Even so, the final selection of information in this book was mine, so I have to take the blame for any errors it contains.

Special thanks go to my colleague Simon Clay, who again chased Capri owners all round the country in the hope of finding the right cars on a day when it wasn't raining. I am also very grateful to the owners of the cars we did photograph for making them available to us, and here they are:

Mk II
Nick Carley	1975 3.0 John Player Special, KUE 240P
Mick Gilbert	1976 2.0 S, MDT 173P
John Ireland	1974 3.0 Ghia, SOW 72N
Richard Langford	1977 1600L, SMK 375S

Mk III
Jon Cristini	1985 Tickford Turbo, C444 HOE
Margaret Elliott	1985 2.0 Laser, C498 EEK
Jeff Cohen	1986 2.0 Laser, D51 PRJ
Terry Garnett	1983 1.6 Calypso, BPR 655Y
Charles Newman	1981 3.0 Ghia, NWL 520W
Mark Smith	1987 280 Brooklands, E280 BFE

Simon's photographs have been supplemented by material from Ford's own public relations archives, from Francis Ellingworth's vast personal collection, and from PVEC (Police Vehicle Enthusiasts' Club) whose archivist Paddy Carpenter has an uncanny knack of finding exactly the pictures I need. There are even a couple of my own photographs in there.

I sincerely hope that you enjoy this book and that, if you've bought it to help in a restoration, it will help you achieve what you're after. However, please bear in mind that dates may in some cases not be precise: whether a model was introduced in May or June was fairly immaterial to Ford at the time. Similarly, remember that Ford was in the business of making cars, and their top priority was to get cars out of the doors, not to stick to a rigidly agreed specification. So if the car you're working on doesn't quite conform to what's in this book, don't be surprised! So saying, if I've got something wrong, I'd be happy to hear about it (and to see the evidence) if you want to write to the publishers.

James Taylor
Oxfordshire, June 2018

FORD CAPRI MK II, 1974-1978

The Base models are very rare among surviving Mk II Capris today, because most enthusiasts want the more glamorous types. This Ford publicity picture shows a 1976 1300 model, with steel disc wheels, no vinyl roof, and only black decals for side decoration.

The Capri Mk II was introduced in February 1974. It was not the best time to have introduced a new sporty car, because the oil crisis that had erupted in autumn 1973 was causing buyers to think twice about sporty cars and not at all about big-engined ones. However, Ford had been planning a second version of its Capri for some time under the codename of Diana, not least because sales of the first-generation car had begun to slide. Yet the company clearly believed that there was still plenty of life in the basic Capri concept; the main difference with this second-generation car was that it was deliberately aimed more at the young family buyer.

Not that the Mk 1 Capri had been unsuitable for families. It was simply that the original car had been famously aimed at the young married man as the car he had always promised himself. With two doors, it was never going to be ideal transport when he started a family, but enough Capri buyers seemed to have managed to get around that minor difficulty and had managed to pretend that the Capri was exactly what the family needed.

In the mean time, fashions in the car market had been changing as well. A new breed of small and agile saloon – the supermini – was scoring major successes, and one of its key features was a hatchback with folding rear seats, which together made for maximum versatility as both passenger-carrier and load-carrier. This exercised an important influence on the second-generation Capri. The sleek coupé shape lent itself ideally to a hatchback configuration, and the Mk II was drawn up with a large upward-opening tailgate, accompanied

FORD CAPRI MK II, 1974-1978

CAPRI MK II MODELS AVAILABLE IN THE UK

February 1974 to Summer 1975

1300 L		
1600 L	1600 XL	1600 GT
		2000 GT
		3000 GT 3000 Ghia

Note: New models were introduced at different times over the summer of 1975; see text.

Summer 1975 to March 1978

1300	1.3 L		
	1.6 L	1.6 GL	1.6 S
		2.0 GL	2.0 S	2.0 Ghia
			3.0 S	3.0 Ghia

on most models by split-fold rear seats, to make it a more practical, versatile proposition.

Although the basic silhouette was the one established by the Mk I Capri, the Mk II was slightly longer, slightly wider, and slightly heavier. It also had sharper and smoother lines, with larger side windows. Bizarrely, despite its looks, the new model was actually slightly less aerodynamic than the one it replaced – a fact which Ford kept well hidden for many years!

There were mechanical revisions as well as the sleek body make-over for the Mk II, but nothing too radical. Larger front brake discs were part of the Mk II package, along with softer suspension, and an alternator replaced the earlier dynamo to ensure that the electrical system could meet demand from the increasing number of electrical accessories that buyers now wanted. The 1.3 litre came with a dynamo unless an alternator was specified at extra cost.

There were five engines at launch, three of them carried over from the old model. Smallest was still the 1300 OHV crossflow type; the mid-range consisted of 1600 and 1600GT Pinto types, together with a 2000 that was now an in-line Pinto engine instead of the old V4; and at the top of the range was the familiar 3-litre V6. Gearboxes were four-speed manuals as standard, with a Ford C3 automatic option on most models.

There was also a much simpler set of specification levels than before. Starting at the bottom, the three levels at launch were L, XL, and GT. So the UK range, all built at Halewood, consisted in 1974 of six models: 1300L, 1600L, 1600XL, 1600GT, 2000GT, and 3000GT.

Richard Langford's 1977 1600L model shows the next step up the model hierarchy, although in fact the L model had been considerably enhanced by that stage of Capri production. The rocker panels are blacked out, there are steel Sports wheels, and the much-liked vinyl roof is present as well.

FACTORY-ORIGINAL FORD CAPRI MK II & MK III

The John Player Special edition in 1975 marked the run-out of the original GT models. This 3.0-litre model belongs to Nick Carley, and carries the distinctive gold decals and gold wheels associated with these cars.

THE US-MODEL MK II CAPRIS

The Mk I Capri had been sold quite successfully in the USA, but the arrival of US-model Mk IIs was delayed, and no 1975 models were sold there. So the first Mercury Capri Mk IIs were 1976 models. These had front turn indicators mounted in the grille, four round sealed-beam headlamps, and "5mph" bumpers with body-colour aprons.

The engines were carried over from the Mk I models, but all were now configured to run on lead-free fuel and had catalytic converters in the exhaust system. There were 2300 Pinto, 2600 V6 and 2800 V6 types, the latter now claimed to deliver 109bhp. The former de luxe interior option pack was now marketed under the Ghia name, and in 1976 there was a special S edition with black or white paint, gold wheels and pin-striping, and an upgraded interior in two-tone beige and black.

Production of Mercury Capris to Federal specifications ended at Cologne in August 1977 after 513,449 had been built. Sales continued into 1978. For 1979, Mercury dealers began selling a new Capri, but this one was based on the US-built Ford Mustang.

The US-model Mercury Capri Mk II was introduced in 1976. They were fitted with these chunky 5mph impact bumpers. This is a 2.8-litre V6 model.

FORD CAPRI MK II, 1974-1978

The S models took over from the GT types for the 1976 model-year. This one is a 2.0 S, belonging to Mick Gilbert. The side decals of the S were clearly based on the successful design used on the John Player Special – although they were not exactly the same.

THE GERMAN MK II CAPRIS

Production of Mk II Capris began at the Cologne factory in February 1974, at the same time as Mk II production was beginning at the Halewood factory in the UK. The nine-model German range consisted of 1300 L, 1300 XL, 1600 L, 1600 XL, 1600 GT, 2300 GT, 2300 Ghia, 3000 GT and 3000 Ghia. In addition, the Cologne factory built a 1300 GT model with the cross-flow engine for sale in France and Italy.

For the 1976 model-year, the last one when Halewood built Capris for the UK market, the changes on the Cologne assembly lines were very much the same as those at Halewood. The main difference was that German-built cars could be had with a 2.3-litre engine that was never available in Capris for Britain.

For the 1977 and 1978 model-years, the German factory would continue to build a much larger range of Capris than was ever seen in British showrooms. So from March 1976, there were three new models that did not go on sale. These were a 54bhp 1.3-litre and a 68bhp 1.6-litre (both with low-compression engines and for Germany only) and a new 98bhp 2-litre model with V6 engine.

As all Capris for the UK market were being built in Germany by this stage, the change to Mk III models occurred at the same time for Germany and the UK, in early 1978.

The German Mk II range included L, XL, GT and Ghia trims.

John Ireland's 1974-model 3.0 Ghia represents the top model of the Capri Mk II range, and here displays its tilt-and-slide sunroof.

The Mk II range was of course also built at Cologne in Germany, with a slightly different engine and trim line-up.

This first UK range lasted only for around 18 months. A few months before the revised 1976 range was introduced, Ford provided a preview of what was in store in the shape of a special-edition derivative of the GT range that arrived in March 1975 and remained in production only until June. This was the John Player Special edition, in black with gold pin-striping and named after the successful JPS Formula 1 racing team that Ford supported. (In some countries the John Player identification was not used, and the all-black cars were known as Midnight or Blackbird editions. Just to confuse the issue, there were some white examples as well.)

The revised 1976 range began to appear over the summer of 1975, spearheaded by a 2.0 S model that replaced the 2000 GT, and by October that year the whole range was in place. There were now five trim levels, as the earlier selection had been swelled by a new entry-level trim (usually described as Base) and by a new top trim called Ghia. Ghia was the name of a prominent Italian coachbuilder that Ford had bought when it fell on hard times in 1970, and over the next few years would be applied to all Ford ranges in Europe to indicate the top level of trim and equipment.

With the 1976-model Capris came some reshuffling of equipment levels, and the five varieties were now known as Base, L, GL (which replaced XL), S (which replaced GT) and Ghia. These names helped to harmonise the Capri range with other European Ford ranges of the time. Engine sizes were also differently expressed, except on the Base models, and for the same reason. So the cumulative effect was that the 1976 Capri model range for the UK consisted of ten models in all. These were the 1300, 1.3 L, 1600, 1.6 L, 1.6 GL, 1.6 S, 2.0 S, 2.0 Ghia, 3.0 S and 3.0 Ghia.

One more set of revisions arrived during the 1976 model-

The black-painted sections for the alloy wheels are an attractive feature that was only found on the 1974 and 1975 model cars.

PRODUCTION FIGURES

The 1974-1976 figures are for UK production only. They were calculated from the original Halewood production logs by Chris Rees and published in his book, *Essential Ford Capri* (Bay View Books, 1997).

	1300/1.3	1600/1.6	2000/2.0	3000/3.0	KD kits	Total
1974	2222	28,880	6133	1042	655	38,932
1975	3158	13,271	2130	213	450	21,225
1976	4030	15,508	6432	1063		27,033
					Total UK build	87,190
1977	5448	35,858	24,991	5555		Note 2
1978	3070	25,248	26,412	4916		Note 3

1 After October 1976, cars for sale in the UK were manufactured in Germany. The figures shown are only for UK-built cars. Overall German production totals for 1977 and 1978 were higher than those shown here because the Cologne plant also produced models with engines not available in the UK.

2 The 1977 figures cannot be compared directly with earlier totals because they show Capri production for all markets.

3 The 1978 figures are for the full calendar year. Mk II Capri production actually ended in March, so the Mk II production figures were probably approximately 25% of the totals shown here.

The high-performance versions of the Capri were quite commonly seen as Police cars in Britain. Despite the Wiltshire registration number, this 1977 Capri 3.0 S belonged to the Sussex Police. (PVEC)

year, when the 1.3-litre and 1.6-litre engines were fitted with Ford's "Sonic Idle" carburettor to reduce fuel consumption in February. At the same time, the availability of the automatic gearbox was widened and tinted glass became standard on most Capris. The only model that could have neither was the entry-level Capri 1300.

As Capri sales had not recovered to their former levels (and indeed they never would), Ford decided to concentrate all assembly at Cologne, which had always supplied the Ghia models from the start of Mk II production; none were built at Halewood. The last Halewood-assembled cars of all were built in October 1976 and all the 1977-model Capris were assembled in Germany. Minor differences included the addition of a front air dam and rear spoiler to the S specification, but the British model line-up was the same as before.

There were no further changes to the mainstream models, although an X Pack of performance options was introduced in August 1977. In March 1978 the facelifted model, generally called the Capri Mk III although not by Ford, was announced at the Geneva Motor Show, and the last of the Mk II models were built in March 1978.

WEIGHTS AND MEASURES

Wheelbase	100.8in (2560mm)	
Front track	53.26in (1353mm)	
Rear track	54.48in (1384mm)	
Length	168.8in (4288mm)	
Width	66.85in (1698mm)	
Height	51.1in (1298mm)	
Wheels	13-inch steel disc with 5-inch rim	
	13-inch steel "sports" with 5-inch rim	
	13-inch seven-spoke alloy with 5½in rim	
	13-inch 12-spoke alloy with 5½in rim	
	13-inch RS four-spoke alloy with 7in rim	
	13-inch RS four-spoke alloy with 7½in rim	
Tyres	6.00 x 13 cross-ply	
	165 SR 13 radial	
	185/70HR13 radial	
	205/60VR13 radial	
	225/60VR13 radial	
Kerb weight	1.3-litre models	2226 lb (1010kg)
	1.6-litre models	2293 lb (1040kg), manual
		2314 lb (1050kg), automatic
	1.6-litre GT/S	2314 lb (1050kg), manual
		2337 lb (1060kg), automatic
	2.0-litre models	2335 lb (1059kg), manual
		2348 lb (1065kg), automatic
	3.0-litre models	2568 lb (1165kg), manual
		2579 lb (1170kg), automatic
0-62mph (0-100 km/h)	1.3-litre models	19.4 sec; 20.0 from Feb 1976
	1.6-litre models	16.4 sec, manual
		18.8 sec, automatic
	1.6 GT/S	13.5 sec, manual
		16.1 sec, automatic
	2.0-litre models	11.1 sec, manual
		12.5 sec, automatic
	3.0-litre models	8.5 sec, manual
		10.5 sec, automatic
Max speed	1.3-litre models	88mph (143km/h)
		85mph (137km/h), Feb 1976
	1.6-litre models	97mph (156km/h), manual
		94mph (151km/h), automatic
	1.6 GT/S	104mph (168km/h), manual
		101mph (163km/h), automatic
	2.0-litre models	107mph (173km/h), manual
		105mph (169km/h), automatic
	3.0-litre models	121mph (196km/h), manual
		118mph (190km/h), automatic

The wheels on this 1978 Strathclyde Police Capri suggest a smaller-engined model. Note how the auxiliary driving lights have been mounted ahead of the radiator grille, while there are blue "police" lights hanging below the front bumper. (PVEC)

CAPRI MK II DETAILS

Please note that it is only possible to provide details of the specification that Ford intended for use on these cars. At the Ford assembly plants, just as in those of other manufacturers, the top priority was always to keep the assembly line going. So if temporary shortages of non-critical parts arose (such as cosmetic items associated only with a particular variant), the practice was to complete the cars without them rather than to stop the line and wait for them to be delivered.

There will therefore inevitably be some cars which deviate from the expected norm and are known to have done so from when they were new. Such cars cannot be considered in any sense "wrong", and nor should anyone pretend that they were "special orders": they are just different from standard through quirks of fate.

BODYSHELL AND PANELS

Front valance panel

All versions of the Capri Mk II have a simple metal valance panel running between the two front wings and bolted to them at each end. On the German-built Capri S models which reached the UK market from November 1976 (but not on the Halewood-built models built between October 1975 and October 1976), a small GRP spoiler is screwed to this. Its purpose was to improve stability at speed. The spoiler is tucked away well under the bodywork and is more readily visible from the side of the car.

Original Capri S spoilers were manufactured in two pieces. A one-piece fibreglass reproduction item has been made available through the Capri Club.

Worth noting is that German-built Capris Mk II cars for markets outside the UK had towing-and-lashing eyes behind the valance panel, and also at the rear. The UK-market cars, however, never did.

Bonnet slam panel

The bonnet slam panel has the receiver for the bonnet catch in its centre, with a spring visible above the panel; this spring was not painted when the cars were new. On the left of the panel, standing in front of the car and looking into the engine bay, is the identification plate, and on the right is a Body Plate that is painted in the body colour. Some cars also have a sticker with a series of E codes next to the identification plate. Note that some slam panels have two pressed "bumps" at each outer end, while others only have one. There is no convincing explanation of why this should have been so, except that perhaps two different pressing plants or perhaps two sets of dies were in use.

The support bracket for the bonnet prop rod is pressed out of the slam panel at the left-hand end, and the rod itself passes through a translucent nylon washer inserted in the bracket. A bend in the rod holds it in place without the need for any additional fixing. When the prop rod is lowered, it is located on the opposite side of the slam panel by a white plastic receiver clip, which is prone to breakage and has therefore sometimes been replaced by a non-original item.

Front inner wings

The front inner wings are painted in the body colour, like the rest of the engine bay. There are two basic types of inner wing, one for the four-cylinder cars and one for the V6 models, and the major difference is that the type for the bigger-engined models has reinforcing plates welded around the tops of the suspension struts and extending a few inches down the inner face of the wing. It was possible to order these reinforced wings for the four-cylinder models as well, although few people did so unless they were intending to use the cars for motorsport events. The wings on V6 models are also braced

The profile of the front spoiler on a 3.0-litre S model is clear in this contemporary Ford publicity picture.

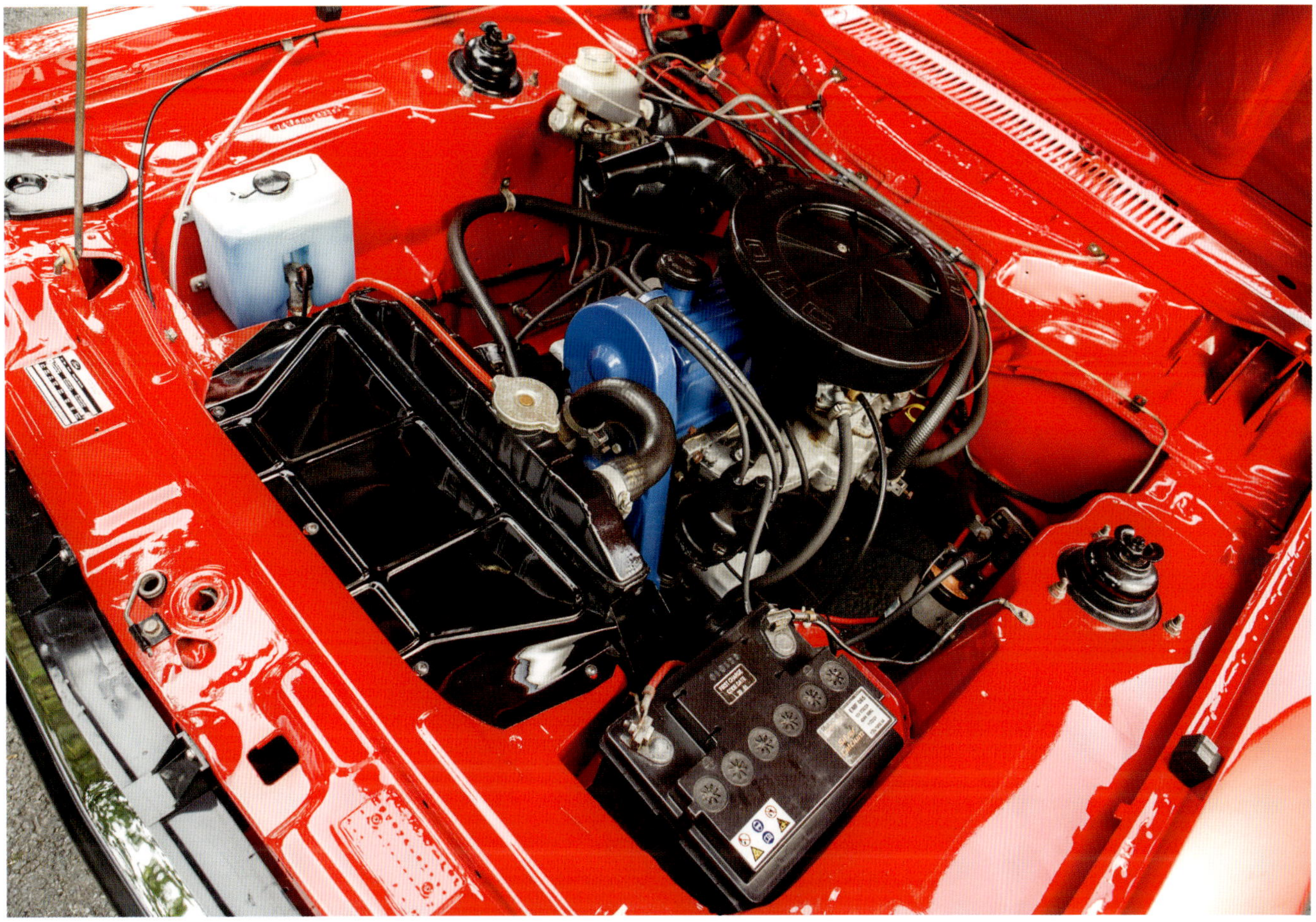

CAPRI MK II DETAILS

This view of the engine bay in a 1.6-litre model shows the bonnet slam panel with its exposed spring in the centre and the triangular pressing that forms the mounting for the prop rod. The car identification plate is next to the prop rod, and just visible at the bottom of the picture is the Body Plate. The access panel for the headlamp is black on this car, and of course there is a long air duct plate between slam panel and radiator because this is a four-cylinder car with a short engine.

The reinforcing plate around the suspension strut mounting is clear in this picture of a 3.0-litre model from 1974. The headlamp access plate is again black and the bonnet buffer has a domed head. Also visible is the cream plastic retaining clip for the bonnet prop rod.

The headlamp access plate on this 1975 Capri S is made of translucent plastic, and is held in place by a single screw. The bonnet buffer is visible ahead of it, in this case having a hollow rather than a domed head.

FACTORY-ORIGINAL FORD CAPRI MK II & MK III

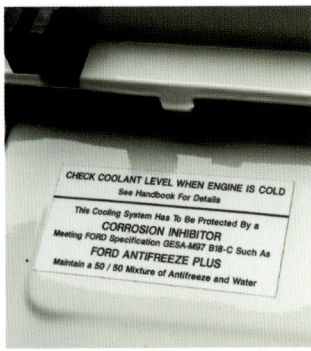

Stickers on the left-hand inner wing of the 3.0-litre car were positioned so that they could be read by someone working on the engine bay.

The underside of the bonnet was always finished in the body colour – in this case black, as the car is a John Player Special model. Also clear here are the positions of the bonnet prop rod and the bonnet release catch.

to the bulkhead by a triangular plate on each side, but this plate is not normally present on the four-cylinder cars.

Nevertheless, small numbers of otherwise standard four-cylinder models have been found with this triangular bracing, but without the reinforcing plates on the inner wings. The probable explanation is that V6 bodyshells were used to keep the assembly line moving when there was a temporary shortage of the four-cylinder type.

At the front of each inner wing is a cut-out section which gives access to the rear of the headlamp. These cutouts are protected by triangular access panels that are each held in place by a single screw into the top of the inner wing. Some of these access panels are made of translucent plastic, and others have a black finish. There is also an adjustable bonnet buffer just in front of each of these access covers, with a round black rubber head.

Front outer wings

As on the Mk I Capri, the front outer wings are single-piece pressings, although obviously not interchangeable with earlier types. They are welded to the main bodyshell. Reproduction panels have been made available, and commonly need a little re-shaping at the rear top, just ahead of the windscreen pillar.

Cars equipped with a radio normally have a chromed telescopic aerial towards the rear of the left-hand front wing, let into the top surface. This was originally a manually-operated item, although some owners have chosen to change to an electrically-operated type.

Bonnet

All the Mk II Capris have the same bonnet panel, which incorporates a small power bulge towards its rear edge. On the first Mk I cars, the power bulge was associated only with the largest (3-litre V6) engine, but customers liked it so much that it was made standard. The same practice was therefore carried over to the Mk II models.

Scuttle panel

The scuttle panel is a simple pressing between the base of the windscreen and the bonnet. Into it are punched a series of openings which allow air to pass through and into the car's heating and ventilating system. There is also a pair of apertures which allow the spindles for the wipers to pass through. The wiper arms are black on all models.

CAPRI MK II DETAILS

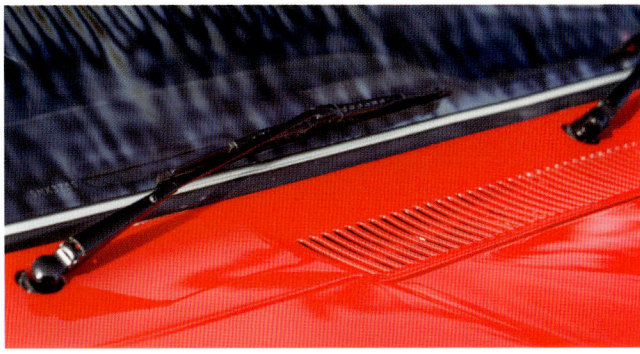

The design of the scuttle panel was broadly similar to that on Mk I Capris: it was a simple pressing with air vents. Wiper arms were black on all models.

The flush-fitting door handles incorporated a keylock and were in bright metal on most models.

Doors

The doors are made in the usual way with a steel outer skin clenched over a steel inner pressing to form the lower section. The upper section consists of a simple steel frame which carries the drop-glass and is inserted into the lower section and bolted in place.

The window frames on the Base 1300, the S models, and on the all-black John Player Special, are finished in satin black. On other models they are chromed, although the rear vertical section is always black to help give the illusion of a larger glass area when the door is closed. On all models except the all-black cars, there is also a bright metal finisher on the horizontal top surface of the door panel at the base of the window aperture.

On most models, the door handles are in bright metal, even where this contrasts with black window frames (as, for example on the S models). Black door handles were used only on the John Player Special edition and its overseas all-black equivalents. Each door handle has its own keylock; on the Halewood-built cars, and on the John Player Special models, the slot for the key is horizontal, but on the German-built cars it is vertical.

For the first year of production, none of the Capri Mk II models had any door mirrors as standard – not even the Ghia – although a driver's door mirror could be had as an optional extra. All this changed in October 1975, when a driver's door mirror became standard with the L trim and above. At this stage, the S and Ghia models also gained a matching mirror for the passenger's door as standard. The driver's door mirror was available at extra cost for the entry-level models, and the passenger door mirror was also available at extra cost for those models which did not have it.

The standard door mirrors had a short stem attached to the door, with a rectangular head that pivoted on this. There was no clamp: the mirror stayed in adjustment through friction in its pivot mounting – or at least, did so until it became too worn. The mirror bodies were finished in bright metal or in satin black as appropriate, to match the window frames on the car.

From October 1975, on the 3.0-litre and Ghia models, the driver's door mirror came with the luxury of a remote adjusting knob mounted on the door trim inside. This would adjust the position of the mirror by means of short cables that passed through the door.

Sports door mirrors were available at extra cost on all models, and these were round with a domed metal body and a long mounting strip that attached to the door. No remotely adjustable version of these mirrors was available.

Window frames were again in bright metal on all models except the entry-level 1300 and the all-black John Player Special.

The standard door mirror is seen here on a 1977 1.6 L model. A black version of the same design was used on entry-level models and on the all-black John Player Special edition.

This was the optional sports mirror, seen here fitted to a 3.0 Ghia model.

19

Floorpan and sills

The floorpan is of course steel and has the transmission tunnel running through it from front to rear. It is made of three sections. The front one includes the transmission tunnel and extends from the engine bay bulkhead to the rear of the passenger compartment. It has longitudinal ribbing on either side of the tunnel, and there are different panels at the front of the transmission tunnel to suit manual or automatic gearboxes. There is a reinforcing cross-member below the front seat mounting position and a second one below the position for the rear seat.

The second section of the floorpan curves up and over the rear axle, and is then welded to the third section, which constitutes the floor of the boot.

At each side, the main floorpan is welded to the body sills, which are an important structural element of the bodyshell. These have an outer panel, an inner panel, and various strengthening sections sandwiched between them. Various repair panels have been available over the years, but in many cases are a poor fit.

As a general rule, the outer sills (sometimes called rocker panels) are painted in satin black, and this paint is continued in a straight line across the lower front wings as well. However, Base and L models had body-colour sills, and in later years the black sills were not available with certain exterior paint colours (see Paint and Trim chart for details). On the Ghia models only, there is an additional bright metal trim strip that runs along the top of the black section.

Roof

A grained vinyl roof covering had been popular on the Mk I Capris and was made available again from the start of Mk II production. It was standard on Ghia models and was listed as an extra-cost option for all others except for the Base 1300. On the S models, it was available only in Black, but on all other models there was a choice. Initially, this was between

This is the sunroof in its closed position. The bright gutters conceal the edges of the vinyl covering, and the division of that covering into separate sections is illustrated here.

Again, the seam between the central section of the vinyl roof cover and the side section is clear here. The later type of plastic washer jet for the tailgate window can also be seen.

Most Capri Mk II models sold in the UK probably had the vinyl roof covering. Here it is on a 3.0 Ghia from 1974, equipped with a tilting sunroof which is seen in the open position.

CAPRI MK II DETAILS

The edge of the vinyl trim on the quarter-pillar is covered by a black metal trim strip.

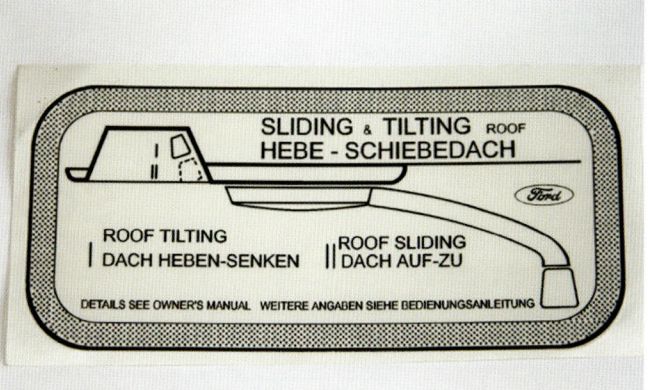

Often missing on cars that have had replacement windscreens (that is, most of them), this is the sticker giving operating instructions for the sunroof. The one pictured is a reproduction item, still on its protective backing paper.

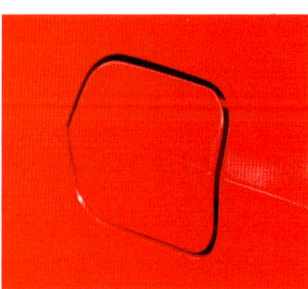

The fuel filler is concealed under a simple hinged flap in the right-hand rear wing panel.

Black and Tobacco, but Brown also became available once production had switched completely to Germany (see the Paint and Trim table on page 28 for further details). All vinyl roofs had matching-colour horizontal finisher strips on the rear body pillars and below the rear window on the tailgate.

The rain gutters ran above the side windows, and were normally painted to match the body. However, cars with a vinyl roof covering had a special gutter covering that was intended to give the appearance of bright metal. This covering is actually transparent plastic, with a bright foil-like insert, and it slides over the guttering on the body. The bright insert tends to yellow with age, and replacement gutter covers are extremely hard to find.

A manually operated tilt-and-slide steel sunroof was standard on Ghia models from the start, and was an extra cost option on other models. When a sunroof was fitted, the sliding panel was trimmed to match the rest of the roof, and the underside of the panel was trimmed to match the head lining.

Rear quarter-panels

The body's rear quarter-panels are integral to the main bodyshell and incorporate the rear roof pillars. There is no decoration on these panels unless the car has side trim strips or a vinyl roof covering. The right-hand panel has a hinged rectangular flap for the fuel filler, low down and close to the body side crease.

Hatchback

The big hatch at the tail of the car is hinged from the roof panel and is supported by a gas strut on each side. There is a combined keylock and press-button release in the centre of the lower section, and these always had a bright metal finish, even when the rest of the brightwork was blacked out (as on Base 1300 models). John Player Special cars were the only exception – they had a blacked-out boot lock.

Ghia models always had a rear wash-wipe system as

The vinyl "roof" also covered the top section of the tailgate, where another black plastic trim strip ensured that it had a neat lower edge.

FACTORY-ORIGINAL FORD CAPRI MK II & MK III

The John Player Special cars were the only models to feature a blacked-out book lock.

The tail hatch was not a feature of Mk I versions of the Capri, but played an important role in making the Mk II models more family-friendly.

The Ford name was displayed across the centre of the hatch, below the press-button release.

The black paint ended abruptly where the rear panel joined the wing on each side.

standard, and this was also available as part of the Sports Custom Pack for the GT from the beginning of Capri Mk II production. It was then standardised on GL and S models as well in October 1975. The spindle of the wiper drive emerges just below the tailgate window and just left of centre, and the wiper arm is always black.

The washer jet is located on the right-hand side of the roof, just above the tailgate aperture. On early cars, this is a round metal item (which is now very hard to find). The later type, introduced probably from October 1975, is made of black plastic.

Tail panel and rear valance

The rear wings wrap around to meet the edges of the tail panel and are welded to it. The tail panel itself lies between hatchback and bumper and carries the rear light units. Between these, it has a recessed centre, where the number-plate is fitted.

The panel is painted in the body colour on Base and L models, but on GL models and above it is in satin black. This paint covers the whole face of the panel, including the top edge, and is not limited to the section that is visible when the hatchback is closed. The number-plate lights (see below) are mounted to the top of the rearward-facing section of this panel.

Note that on the Capri S, the side decal kit does not run across the tail panel but finishes with a vertical section at the edge of each rear wing. By contrast, the striping on the John Player Special models continues across the top and bottom of the tail panel.

The rear valance panel is the same on all models of Capri Mk II. It is arranged to finish above the lower edges of the rear wings, so that there is room on either side for an exhaust tailpipe in the "corner" that the join between the panels creates. This suits both four-cylinder cars with the single tailpipe and V6 models with one tailpipe on each side.

The rear panel around the number-plate and tail lights was normally painted in the body colour, as on this 1977 1.6 L model.

The rear panel was blacked out on more expensive models, such as this 3.0 Ghia.

CAPRI MK II DETAILS

Most models have bumpers with a bright metal finish and a black rubber bump strip. This is the front bumper of a 1977 1.6 L model...

... and this is the rear bumper of the same car.

On Ghia models, the grille had a bright rim and a pair of bright-finish "spears" around the Ford name.

BODY FITTINGS

Bumpers

Both front and rear bumpers are single-piece items made of steel. On the entry-level 1300 models, they are coated in matt black polyester, and these bumpers are also fitted to the mid-range S models. The all-black John Player Special cars have a version of these bumpers with a black rubber bump-strip. That bump-strip is standard on all other models, where the bumpers are bright metal rather than black. On the Ghia models, there are additionally black over-riders which are made of solid rubber. Similar over-riders were part of the early Sports Custom Pack as well.

The front number-plate is bolted to brackets hanging down from a recess in the centre of the bumper.

Radiator grille

The radiator grille is a simple metal frame with a cross-hatch of wires attached to it. On all models it is painted black and carries the Ford name in separate letters across the centre. These letters have black plastic bodies and chromed faces.

On the GT and Ghia models, there is a chromed plastic frame to the grille, with joins between its two halves covered by very noticeable sliding clips. The GT and Ghia versions of the grille also have a chromed horizontal "spear" on either side of the Ford name badge.

There was a special version of the grille for the John Player Special cars, where both the Ford letters and the grille frame were painted in gold to match the side-stripe decals and wheel detailing.

Glass and glazing

Clear glass was standard from the beginning with all levels of trim except Ghia, which always came with green tinted glass all round as standard. The tinted glass was available as an extra-

All-black bumpers without the rubber bump strip were standard for the entry-level models and, as here, the S models as well. The standard radiator grille was always black, with the Ford name in a contrasting bright finish.

Ghia models added black rubber over-riders, front and rear, to the bright metal bumpers.

On the Capri S, the special S decal was the same height as the 2.0 numerals.

The transverse elements of the heated rear window did not cover the full depth of the glass, but would clear enough of an area to give good rearward visibility. Also seen here is the rear wiper arm, which was black like those at the front.

Engine size was displayed in large numerals on each front wing. Except with the 1.3-litre engine, the numerals had a bright metal finish.

The white paint on this 3.0 Ghia helps to emphasise that the sides of the numerals were finished in black.

cost option on all other models, except for the Base 1300.

The standard windscreen was always made of toughened "safety" glass, but a laminated type was an extra-cost option from the start of production on all models. On cars fitted with a sunroof, there was always a decal on the inside of the windscreen, just behind the rear view mirror, giving operating instructions for the sunroof. Reproductions of this decal have been made available. A heated rear window was standard with all trim levels except L before October 1975, when it became a standard fitment on all models except the 1300. It eventually became standard on the 1300 as well in September 1976.

All the glass in a Mk II Capri is rubber-glazed to the bodywork, except the opening rear quarter-lights on Ghia models (see below), which sit against a rubber seal when closed.

Rear quarter-windows

The rear quarter-windows were actually made larger than those on Mk I Capris, to counter complaints of poor visibility out of the rear seat. Nevertheless they retained the horseshoe shape that had been so much liked on the original models.

These windows have their own frames, which match the bright metal or satin-black frames on the doors' drop-glasses. However, the front vertical section of the frame is always in satin black, even on bright metal frames, to match the trailing edge of the frame around the door drop-glass and to contribute to the visual impression of a large and uninterrupted side glass area.

On most Capri Mk II models, these rear side windows are fixed, but on the Ghia models they can be opened. These opening windows appear never to have been available as an option on other models of the Mk II Capri. There is a pair of hinges attached to the leading (straight) edge of the glass, and a hinged arm at the rear limits the amount by which the rear of the glass can be pushed outwards. This hinged arm is attached through a hole in the glass, and the attachment is concealed by a circular bright metal finisher on the outside of the window.

Body side trims

The styling of the Capri Mk II depended on creases in the body panels, and was designed to look attractive without the complication of external decoration. Nevertheless, such decoration was used on several models.

At the bottom end of the model hierarchy, the entry-level 1.3-litre cars have a black twin coachline decal running just above the lower body side crease between the rear of the front wheelarch and the front of the rear wheelarch. With the Ghia trim there was always a bump strip along the upper body crease, and this wrapped around the rear of the car to cover the tailgate as well. This rubbing strip was also made standard on GL models from October 1975.

A decal package was also introduced during 1975, appearing initially on the John Player Special models (and their equivalents outside the UK). A slightly different version then became standard on models with the S trim. Both types were applied to the lower body sides and created a "frame" effect from twin coachlines, thick on the outside and thin on the inside. The decals were available in various colours and on the S models the colour was carried over to the S decals on the front wings. Note that these decal striping kits have been unavailable new for some time and that although some versions have been reproduced, most of the reproduction decals available for Capris are for Mk III models.

CAPRI MK II DETAILS

The Ghia badge was more ornate than other model type badges. Once again, the white paint helps to show that the sides of these badges were black.

On the tailgate, the Capri badge was applied across the middle of a red "II" decal. The model type, in this case L, was then displayed next to it.

On the Capri S, or John Player Special, the model designation was in its usual place, but the letter was painted black to match the bodywork.

Front wing badges

The story of the front wing badges divides into two, because the 3-litre Ghia models had different arrangements from the other models. On the majority of models, the front wing badges on the first season's cars were the same as those used on the final Mk I cars. They were shield-type badges that were mounted just behind each front wheelarch. All follow the same basic design, with a black strip at the top that shows the engine size, and a red lower portion which has several different configurations. These badges show engine size only, and do not differentiate between L, XL and GT trim levels.

On 1300 models, the lower red portion of the shield has no additional elements. On 1600 and 2000 models, the red portion of the shield has a silver diagonal stripe. On the 3000GT models, the red lower portion carries V6 identification, with the 6 sitting above the V.

These badges lasted only until October 1975, and the later type was previewed on the John Player Special models that marked the end of 2000 GT production earlier in the year. These later models (which were 1976 model-year and later types) have large metal numerals on each front wing, reading "1.3", "1.6", "2.0" or "3.0" as appropriate. However, numerals with a matt black finish were used for the entry-level 1.3-litre model.

The S models have a large S decal next to the engine size badge, in one of several colours to contrast with the main body colour and to match the side lining decals. For details of these colours, please see the Paint and Trim table on page 28.

The 3-litre Ghia was different, and had large metal "3.0" numerals on each front wing from the start. These numerals are held to the wing by pins on their rear faces, and have black-finished edges to help them stand out against the paintwork. They are mounted lower down the wing than the later engine-capacity numerals. From October 1975, a small Ghia shield badge was added above the "3.0" numerals; this has a red and blue enamelled face and was again attached by pins. Some later cars have a plastic version of this badge that was glued in place, but the metal badge continued in use until at least late 1977, and it may be that the two types were used interchangeably as production of the Mk II drew to a close.

Rear badges

The tailgate carries FORD identification on its lower edge, below the release button. The letters are the usual Ford type made of bright metal with black sides to create an additional contrast.

However, the major badges at the rear of the Mk II Capri are carried on the right of the tailgate, towards the lower edge. Central to these is a red decal "II" (indicating Mk II), and mounted across it is the word Capri. This is in block capital letters that are made from metal but have black-painted sides. They attached to the panel by pins on their rear faces. Note that the red "II" decal was sometimes absent from 1977 and 1978 cars, no doubt as a result of shortages on the lines, but that it did continue in use until the end of production.

Model designation badges are then mounted to the right of this badge cluster. They consist of the letters L, XL, GL, S or Ghia, as appropriate (and there is obviously no extra badge on entry-level Capris). All these badges are again made from metal with black-finished sides, except for the S badge, which is finished in satin black to match the bumpers and blacked-out window frames of those models. All badges except the Ghia type are attached by pins on their rear faces; the Ghia type is glued in place.

Cars fitted with an automatic gearbox have an "Automatic" badge on the left of the tailgate, again with unpainted metal faces for the letters and black-painted side sections.

When appropriate, there was an "Automatic" badge on the left-hand side of the tailgate. This one is on a John Player Special 3.0-litre car, and is one of the few items that retained its bright finish on those models.

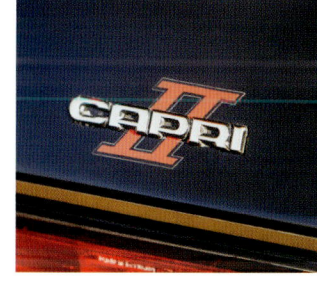

There was no trim level badge on the John Player Special cars.

The headlights were always Lucas Halogen H4 units, and the front direction indicators were mounted separately from them. The lenses of the direction indicators were handed.

LIGHTING

Headlights and sidelights

Like the Mk I models, the Mk II Capris have rectangular headlight units. These units are however specific to the Mk II models, and are noticeably larger than those on the Mk Is. They have no bezels. Their design was apparently by Peter Stevens, who later became a well-known freelance car designer. Sidelight bulbs are contained within the main headlight units.

The headlamps on lower-specification models are sealed-beam types. Halogen H4 headlamps were standard on Ghia models from the start of production, and were an extra-cost option on L and XL models. From October 1975, they were also made standard on the GL models that replaced the XL types in the Capri range.

A headlamp wash-wipe system was never made available for UK-market cars, although it could be had on versions of the Capri Mk II sold on the European continent. The headlamps on these models have moulded "pips" at the tops and bottoms of their lenses to prevent the wiper blades overshooting.

Front direction indicators

The amber direction indicator lamps are mounted outboard of each headlamp, and are handed. Like the headlights, these light units have no decorative bezels.

Auxiliary lighting

Auxiliary lighting generally seems to have been fairly uncommon on the Mk II Capri, although Ford did offer both auxiliary forward-facing fog lamps (from the start of Mk II production) and auxiliary long-range lamps (from July 1977) as accessories. One reason for their relative lack of popularity must have been that no such lamps were ever standard on any of the showroom-specification models. There was therefore no incentive for owners of lesser types to dress up their cars to look like the more expensive or better-equipped versions.

The auxiliary fog lamps had a peaked frame, and were normally mounted in pairs on specially shaped brackets bolted to the front valance, some distance below the bumper. The auxiliary long-range lamps were rectangular types with no frame, the glass being bonded directly to the bowl; they were made by Hella and were mounted on top of the bumper, again with the aid of special brackets.

Rear lights

The rear light units have a clean, rectangular design that is very much in keeping with the clean lines of the rest of the Mk II body. Reversing lights were always standard and were incorporated within these light units. The plastic lens assemblies are held to the backplates by four cross-head setscrews.

The twin number-plate lights have chromed plastic housings

The neat rectangular tail lights incorporated reversing light segments, as well as stop, tail, reflector and direction indicator.

CAPRI MK II DETAILS

Twin number-plate lamps were normally concealed under the closed hatchback.

with integral lenses. They are mounted at the top of the tail panel above the number-plate, and are normally invisible because they are concealed by the overhanging edge of the tailgate.

It was also possible to buy auxiliary red fog guard lamps, which were rectangular items that came with special brackets to allow these lamps to be bolted to the rear valance below the bumper.

ELECTRICAL

The electrical system on all Mk II Capris is a 12-volt type with a negative earth.

Battery and charging system

The battery is mounted in the engine bay, on the left-hand side of the car (the right as you stand looking into the engine bay). The 1.3-litre and 1.6-litre models had a 38 amp-hour type when new, but the 2.0-litre and 3.0-litre cars were supplied with a 44 amp-hour type to match their generally higher levels of electrical equipment and the higher starting loads on the battery.

The 1.3-litre Capris came as standard with a dynamo to charge the battery, but an alternator was available from the beginning at extra cost. Other models always came with an alternator. On cars built at Halewood, this was usually a Lucas 15ACR type, with an output of 28 amps, but a Lucas 17ACR could also be fitted, with a higher 35-amp rating.

On German-built cars, the alternators were usually by Bosch or Femsa. The standard Bosch type was a model G1 with a 28-amp output, although a type K1 could be fitted as an alternative, with a 35-amp or (exceptionally) a 55-amp output. The Femsa alternator always had the same 32-amp rating.

Windscreen wipers and washers

Wiper arms are invariably black, and are arranged to park on the passenger's side of the windscreen. This means that the arrangements for LHD and RHD cars differ. An intermittent wiper control became standard on all models when the three-stalk ISO arrangement for the steering column was introduced in October 1976.

The washer jets are more or less invisible on the surface, and are in fact the flattened ends of copper tubes which have their top surfaces level with the metal of the air intake grille in the scuttle. Each tube is bolted to the bulkhead and attaches to the plastic washer tubing at the lower end. The flattened ends were always a rather unsatisfactory arrangement and often become blocked.

Horns

A single-tone horn was standard on low-specification models, but the Capri S and Capri Ghia both had a pair of horns as standard, one with a high note and one with a low note.

A pair of air horns seems to have been available as an optional extra from the start of Mk II Capri production, but they were very rare on cars sold in the UK

This picture gives a very clear idea of the underbonnet layout on a four-cylinder Capri Mk II, in this case a 1977 1.6 L model. The brake servo and master cylinder are at top left (this is a right-hand-drive car), the washer reservoir is at bottom left, the coil on the left-hand inner wing (on the right of this picture), and the battery at bottom right. The cap of the brake fluid reservoir is translucent.

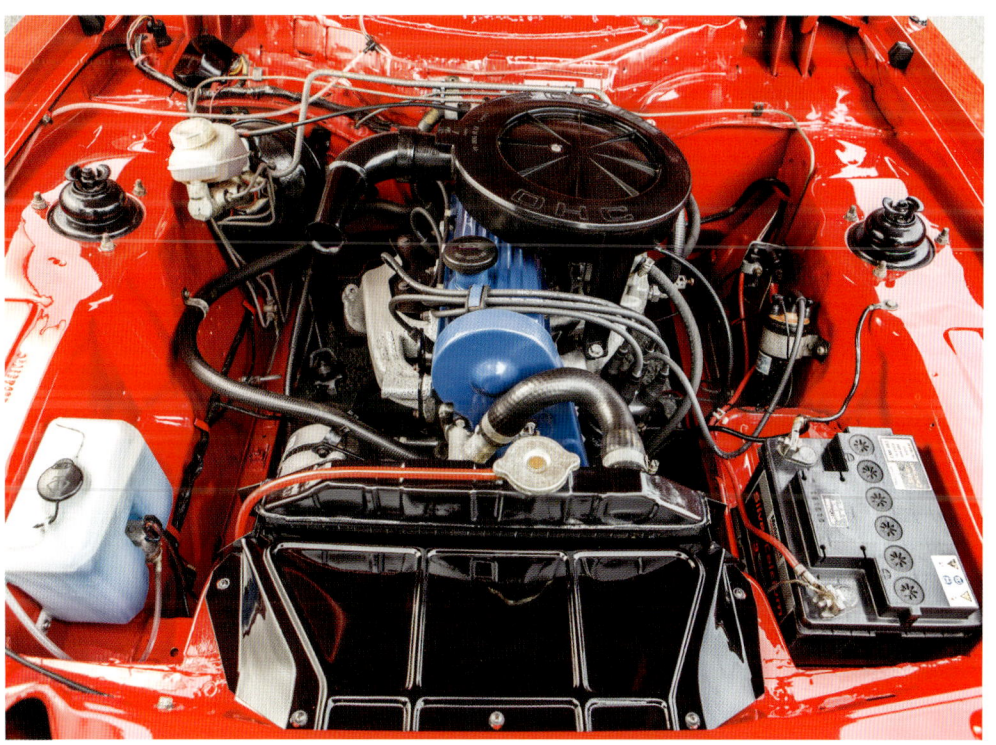

> **THE SPORTS CUSTOM PACK**
>
> At the start of Capri Mk II production, a Sports Custom Pack was made available for the GT models. This consisted of sports road wheels (the steel disc type were standard), a double body side stripe, over-riders, a rear wash-wipe system and a map reading lamp.

PAINTS AND TRIMS, CAPRI MKII

The paint colour code is shown on a sticker attached to the boot floor to the left of the spare wheel well. The sticker shows the paint name, paint code and paint supplier's name.

Occasionally, a paint code sticker like this one remains on the car, although many have probably worn off or been removed over time.

October 1975 Coachlines
These were used on L and S models, in different styles.

Solid colours	L models	S models
Black	(N/A)	Black,
Black	(N/A)	Gold
Carnival Red	White	Black
Diamond White	Black	Black
Daytona Yellow	Black	Black
Laurel Green	White	Black
Olympic Blue	Black	Black
Royal Blue	Gold	Gold
Sahara Beige	Black	Black
Signal Orange	Black	Black
Metallic colours	**L models**	**S models**
Arizona Gold	Black	Black
Green Jade	Black	Black
Miami Blue	White	Black
Platinum	Black	Black
Purple Velvet	White	White
Roman Bronze	Gold	Gold

June 1974
There were eight solid colours and six metallic options. The metallic options cost extra. A vinyl roof covering was standard on Ghia models but optional on others.

The upholstery in L models was vinyl; in XL and GT models it combined vinyl and fabric. Note that the Tan colour used in this period ("Light Tan 73" to Ford) is not the same as the Tan used on 1976 and later models.

The combinations were as follows.

Solid colours	Interior (L, XL and GT)	Interior (Ghia)	Vinyl roof
Daytona Yellow	Black or Saddle	Black, Cloud or Tan	Black or Tobacco
Diamond White	Black or Saddle	Black, Cloud or Tan	Black or Tobacco
Marine Blue	Marquis or Saddle	Black, Cloud or Tan	Black
Modena Green	Black or Tan	Black, Cloud or Tan	Black
Olympic Blue	Black or Marquis	Black, Cloud or Tan	Black
Sahara Beige	Saddle or Tan	Black or Tan	Black or Tobacco
Sebring Red	Black or Saddle	Black, Cloud or Tan	Black or Tobacco
Sunset Red	Black or Tan	Black, Cloud or Tan	Black
Metallic colours			
Copper Brown	Black or Tan	Black, Cloud or Tan	Black or Tobacco
Flame Orange	Black or Saddle	Black, Cloud or Tan	Black or Tobacco
Miami Blue	Black or Marquis	Black, Cloud or Tan	Black
Onyx Green	Saddle or Tan	Black, Cloud or Tan	Black
Purple Velvet	Black or Tan	Black, Cloud or Tan	Black
Stardust	Black or Marquis	Black, Cloud or Tan	Black or Tobacco

October 1975
There were nine solid colours and six metallic options. The metallic options cost extra, as did Signal Orange. Black was available only on S models and at extra cost.

The vinyl roof covering was not available on the 1300 models. A Tobacco vinyl roof was not available on S models and was not available with Diamond White when the Cloud trim was specified.

S models in Carnival Red were not available with Cloud trim.

There were four interior colours in this period: Black, Chocolate, Cloud, Marquis and Tan. Note that the Tan used in this period ("Light Tan 76" to Ford) is not the same as the Tan used on earlier Mk II Capris.

Solid colours	Interior (L and GL)	Interior (S and Ghia)	Vinyl roof
Black	(N/A)	Black, Cloud or Tan	Black
Carnival Red	Black or Tan	Black, Cloud or Tan	Black
Diamond White	Black or Tan	Black, Cloud or Tan	Black or Tobacco
Daytona Yellow	Black or Chocolate	Black or Tan	Black
Laurel Green	Black or Tan	Black or Tan	Black
Olympic Blue	Black or Marquis	Black, Cloud or Tan	Black
Royal Blue	Black or Marquis	Black, Cloud or Tan	Black
Sahara Beige	Black or Chocolate	Black or Tan	Black or Tobacco
Signal Orange	Black or Chocolate	Black or Tan	Black
Metallic colours			
Arizona Gold	Black or Chocolate	Black or Tan	Black or Tobacco
Green Jade	Black or Tan	Black, Cloud or Tan	Black
Miami Blue	Black or Marquis	Black, Cloud or Tan	Black
Platinum	Black or Marquis	Black, Cloud or Tan	Black
Purple Velvet	Black or Tan	Black, Cloud or Tan	Black
Roman Bronze	Black or Tan	Black or Tan	Black or Tobacco

October 1976

There were 13 exterior paint colours, of which seven were extra-cost metallics or "signal" colours. A vinyl roof covering was available, in either Black or Brown.

Three interior colours were available on all models – Night Black, Safari Brown and Tuareg Blue. A fourth (Earth Brown) was available on all models except for Ghia types, and a fifth (Rock Grey) was available on Ghia models only. Standard upholstery was in cloth with a pattern of rectangles. Standard Ghia upholstery was in Rialto cloth with a striped pattern, and with vinyl bolsters. Grained leather upholstery could be had at extra cost on L, XL and GT models.

The combinations were as follows.

Solid colours	Interior	Vinyl roof	Notes
Daytona Yellow (Code T)	Earth Brown	Black or Brown	Not Ghia
	Night Black	Black or Brown	
	Safari Brown	Black or Brown	
Diamond White (Code XSC691A)	Earth Brown	Black or Brown	Not Ghia
	Night Black	Black or Brown	
	Rock Grey	Black	Ghia only
	Safari Brown	Black or Brown	
	Tuareg Blue	Black	Not Ghia
Olympic Blue	Night Black	Black	
	Rock Grey	Black	Ghia only
	Safari Brown	Black	
	Tuareg Blue	Black	
Royal Blue	Night Black	Black	
	Rock Grey	Black	Ghia only
	Safari Brown	Black	
	Tuareg Blue	Black	
Sahara Beige	Earth Brown	Black or Brown	Not Ghia
	Night Black	Black or Brown	
	Safari Brown	Black or Brown	
Spanish Red	Earth Brown	Black or Brown	Not Ghia
	Night Black	Black or Brown	
	Rock Grey	Black	Ghia only
	Safari Brown	Black or Brown	

Special colours	Interior	Vinyl roof	Notes
Arizona Gold (met)	Earth Brown	Black or Brown	Not Ghia
	Night Black	Black or Brown	
	Safari Brown	Black or Brown	
Mediterranean Green (met)	Earth Brown	Black	Not Ghia
	Night Black	Black	
	Rock Grey	Black	Ghia only
	Safari Brown	Black	
Miami Blue (met)	Night Black	Black	
	Rock Grey	Black	Ghia only
	Safari Brown	Black	
	Tuareg Blue	Black	
Montana Brown (met)	Earth Brown	Black or Brown	Not Ghia
	Night Black	Black or Brown	
	Safari Brown	Black or Brown	
Polar Silver (met)	Earth Brown	Black	Not Ghia
	Night Black	Black	
	Rock Grey	Black	Ghia only
	Safari Brown	Black	
	Tuareg Blue	Black	Not Ghia
Signal Green (met)	Earth Brown	Black	Not Ghia
	Night Black	Black	
	Safari Brown	Black	
Signal Orange	Earth Brown	Black or Brown	Not Ghia
	Night Black	Black or Brown	
	Safari Brown	Black or Brown	

March 1977

All the exterior colour options, and most of the interior choices remained unchanged in March 1977, although there was a change of upholstery for the S models. These now had striped Cadiz cloth with black vinyl bolsters; the cloth was available in the four colours of Green, Grey, Orange, and Tan, of which Green seems to have been by far the rarest.

October 1977

Most of the colours listed below were probably introduced as early as August 1977. Trim colours remained unchanged from the previous season, but from October 1977, the Orange interior colour option was dropped.

The paint options available in the final year of Capri Mk II production are not established for certain, but they appear to have been as listed below. Please treat this list with caution. Note that a small number of very late Capri Mk II models were probably painted in colours associated with the incoming Mk III models. In the list that follows, Ford's XSC paint codes are shown in brackets.

Standard colours

Bermuda Blue	(XSC 942)
Laurel Green	(XSC 1137)
Neptune Blue	(XSC 1057)
Tropic Green	(XSC 1055)
Venetian Red	(XSC 1138)

Extra-cost options

Aquarius Green metallic	(XSC1071)
Black	(XSC 632)
Jupiter Red metallic	(XSC 1087)
Oyster Gold metallic	(XSC1203)
Roman Bronze	(XSC 989)
Saturn Gold	(XSC 978A)
Signal Orange	(XSC 1064)
Signal Yellow	(XSC1034)
Strato Silver	(XSC1056)

The OHC Pinto engines all had blue-painted timing covers and rocker covers and, in this case, the legend "Ford OHC" was clearly marked on the air cleaner. The multi-blade cooling fan is yellow. The air intake trumpet could be rotated downwards to pick up warm air from the exhaust manifold to aid warm-up in cold conditions.

ENGINE, FUEL SYSTEM AND EXHAUST

Five engines were available in UK-built Capri Mk II models, and the same five engines were available in German-built Capris for the UK market after October 1976. The entry-level Capri continued with the 1.3-litre four-cylinder OHV Kent engine that had powered the entry-level Mk I models. The mid-range cars had 1.6-litre OHC four-cylinder Pinto types in standard and GT forms, and a 2.0-litre Pinto engine replaced the old Essex V4 of similar capacity. The fifth engine was the 3.0-litre Essex V6, again carried over from the Mk I models.

Every engine was mounted to a metal support beam bolted across the car below the engine bay. This beam carries the main engine mountings and insulating rubbers, and to those mountings are bolted additional brackets to suit the engine installed in the car.

1.3-litre Kent engines

The 1.3-litre OHV Kent engine is a crossflow type with five main bearings and the combustion chambers in the piston crowns. It has the same dimensions as in Mk I models, with a displacement of 1298cc from an 80.98mm bore and a 62.99mm stroke. The first engines had a 9.0:1 compression ratio with 54bhp but as part of the general range realignment and upgrade in October 1975 the compression was raised to 9.2:1 and power was then quoted as 57bhp at 5500rpm with torque of 67 lb ft at 3000rpm.

As on Mk I 1300 engines, the carburettor is a Ford-manufactured 34mm single-choke type. Three different versions were used, with identifying numbers 711W-9510-RC, 761F-9510-AA, and 71HF-9510-KDA. From February 1976 the so-called Sonic Idle carburettor was introduced to reduce fuel consumption, but it also reduced power to just 50bhp at 5500rpm with 64 lb ft of torque at 3000rpm. This new carburettor was a Motorcraft GPD type with one of two identifying numbers, which were 761F-9510-KBA/KTA and 771F-9510-KBA/KTA. All of these carburettors have a manual choke.

1.6-litre Pinto engines

The 1.6-litre Pinto engine was another carry-over from the Mk I Capri, and was a belt-driven overhead-camshaft four-cylinder from the Pinto family. It has five main bearings and the combustion chambers are in the cylinder head. It was available in both standard and GT states of tune. The GT version was used in both the 1600 GT that was available in 1974-1975 and in the 1.6 S that was available subsequently. All these engines have a blue-painted timing cover.

The standard 1.6-litre engines all had a 9.2:1 compression

CAPRI MK II DETAILS

The blue colour coding for the OHC engine was extended to the plastic air filter box on versions with a twin-choke carburettor. This is the 2.0-litre Pinto engine in a Capri S model. The overall underbonnet layout is the same as with the 1.6-litre engine.

Pictured from the other side, the 2.0-litre engine shows its swivelling air intake trumpet, and how this could be simply moved to pick up warm air from the exhaust manifold. The cap of the brake reservoir is white in this case.

ratio and a 36mm Motorcraft carburettor. Power was 76bhp at 5500rpm and torque was 86.8 lb ft at 2700rpm. A Sonic Idle carburettor was fitted from February 1976, and this resulted in lower power and torque figures as well as supposedly improved fuel consumption. The standard engines all have a blue rocker cover to match the blue timing cover, and they have a black circular air cleaner which is prominently branded "Ford OHC". These engines have a manual choke.

The GT version of the engine has the same 9.2:1 compression but uses a Weber 32/36DGAV carburettor with twin sequential chokes. This originally had 26/27mm choke jets, 140/150 main jets and 55/45 idle jets. From 1976 the main jets were changed to 130/125 size to reduce fuel consumption. All these engines have an automatic choke. The 1.6-litre GT engine has a four-branch tubular exhaust manifold and delivers 88bhp at 5700rpm in standard tune, with torque of 92 lb ft at 4000rpm. It also has a large box-like air cleaner housing made of blue plastic.

The 2000 Pinto engine

The 2.0-litre version of the belt-driven OHC Pinto engine was new to the Capri range with the Mk II models, where it was only ever available in its "GT" tune. Both the timing cover and rocker cover are painted blue, and the engine is

FACTORY-ORIGINAL FORD CAPRI MK II & MK III

Although the overall underbonnet layout with the V6 engine is the same, there are important differences. Note the shorter air duct ahead of the radiator, and the metal fan cowl behind it. The radiator itself is also very noticeably thicker than the one in the four-cylinder cars, while the battery had a branded Ford cover. At the back of the engine bay, on the right of the picture, can be seen the triangular bracing between inner wing and bulkhead that was used only on 3-litre cars; it has a counterpart on the opposite side. Both inner wings also have the reinforcing plates around the suspension strut mounts that were characteristic of the 3-litre Capri. The cover over the battery was not a standard feature.

From this angle, the thicker radiator is even more obvious, and it is clear that the multi-blade cooling fan is yellow. The air intake is fixed and picks up warm air from the left-hand manifold only, and the whole top of the engine is finished in black.

surmounted by the same type of blue plastic air cleaner casing that is seen on the 1.6-litre GT engines.

These engines have a swept volume of 1993cc, achieved from a 90.82mm bore and a 76.95mm stroke. There are five main bearings and the combustion chambers are in the cylinder head. The compression ratio is 9.2:1 and the factory-fit carburettor is a Weber 32/36DGAV, with an automatic choke. In standard tune, maximum power of 98bhp is developed at 5500rpm, and peak torque is 111 lb ft at 3500rpm. Bizarrely, the 2.0-litre engine did not have a tubular exhaust manifold, instead having a less efficient design that was presumably intended to look good.

The 3-litre V6

The all-iron Essex OHV V6 engine was yet another carry-over from the Mk I Capri. First seen in Ford's large saloon models in the mid-1960s, it remained the largest car engine manufactured by the European division of the company when the Mk II Capri entered production. The engine was designed by Ford in Britain, and was named the Essex type after the county where Ford's Dagenham engineering headquarters were situated.

The Essex V6 has a 60-degree angle between cylinder banks and a cross-plane crankshaft that runs in four main bearings. There are large main journals and a heavy flywheel to smooth the power delivery. The pistons have a Heron-head design which was designed to make changes of compression ratio easy to accommodate: all that was needed was an alteration to the depth of the bowl in the piston crown. In its 3-litre form, the V6 has a 93.67mm bore and a 72.42mm stroke. A point of visual recognition is that the distributor is always mounted at the front of these engines, in contrast to the rear mounting position of the later German-built "Cologne" V6 engines (as used, for example in the 2.8-litre Mk III Capri and some US-market versions of the Mk II).

As installed in the Capri Mk II, the Essex V6 has an 8.9:1 compression ratio and a Weber 38/27DGAS carburettor with twin synchronous chokes. The jets are 27mm for the choke, 145 for the main jet and 45 for the idle jet. The main jet was reduced to a 142 size in 1976 (probably in February) to improve fuel consumption, and at the same time the distributor was changed from a Motorcraft 762F to a Bosch type. All these carburettors have an automatic choke. All Essex V6 engines in the Mk II Capri have black rocker covers and a black circular pressed metal air cleaner with its air pick-up tube permanently located just above the left-hand exhaust manifold.

Standard engine outputs are 138bhp at 5100rpm with 174 ft lb at 3000rpm. The engine could be uprated with the X Pack options that were introduced in autumn 1977, when power rose to 175bhp at 5000rpm and torque to 194 lb ft at 4000rpm.

The triangular brace between bulkhead and inner wing is very apparent here, and the fuse box with its black plastic cover is prominent behind it. The brake fluid reservoir on this 1974 car has a red cap.

Fuel system

The fuel tank in the Mk II Capri is mounted in the floor of the boot, behind the rear seat, and is low enough down that a nearly flat load floor can be created when the rear seat is folded forwards. The tank itself holds 12.7 gallons (58 litres) of fuel, although Ford usually described it as a 13-gallon tank. Early tanks have the fuel gauge sender unit inaccessibly located at the back (ie nearer the front of the car). The sender was later moved to a more accessible position at the side of the tank; the exact date of the change is not certain but it was probably October 1975.

Fuel is delivered to the engine on all standard models by a mechanical diaphragm-type pump. The only time an electric fuel pump was used was with the uprated 3.0-litre engine in the X Pack cars.

Exhaust

Although the focus here is on the original exhaust systems as supplied with the cars when they were new, it is important to recognise that aftermarket "sports" or "performance" exhausts have been available for many years. Some of these systems were contemporary with the cars, so although they cannot be considered as "factory original", they may therefore in some cases be considered as "period original".

All the four-cylinder engines were fitted when new with a single-pipe exhaust system that terminates in a silencer with a single outlet pipe on the left side of the car. However, there are differences in the system from one model to another. The 3-litre V6 models have a full-length twin-pipe system with an exhaust tailpipe on either side of the car. (Note that the Mk I Capri had a much more restrictive system which incorporated a cross-over pipe and terminated in a single tail silencer with

Exhausts exited on the left-hand side, except with the V6 engine. This one is on a 1.6 model.

This is the tail pipe of a 2.0 model, with straight exit pipe.

The V6 models had twin exhaust pipes, one on either side of the car. On the Ghia models like this one, those exhausts had chromed tips.

> **ENGINE IDENTIFICATION**
>
> Engine numbers have a two-letter prefix plus a five-digit serial number that matches the car's chassis number. The two-letter prefix is a date code, and can be interpreted by using the date codes shown in Appendix A. So (for example) a TU prefix would indicate an engine built in February 1977.
>
> The engine number is die-stamped into a raised casting on the cylinder block on the right-hand side of all engines (left-hand side when standing looking into the engine bay).

twin outlet pipes that were mainly of cosmetic value.)

The four-cylinder exhausts all consist of three sections. There is a front or down pipe from the manifold, and the 1.3, 1.6, 1.6 GT (1.6S) and 2.0 engines all have different types. There is then a centre silencer and pipe; the 1.3 type differs from the 1.6 type (which is common to both standard and GT versions of the engine), and this in turn differs from the 2.0 type. The third section is the back silencer box with associated pipe and the tailpipe; all 1.6 and 2.0 engines share the same item, but the 1.3 type is different. The GT models always had a bright tailpipe finisher.

The exhaust for the 3.0-litre engine has pipework running along each side of the chassis from the exhaust manifolds, with a main silencer on each side. There is then a final section of pipework on each side with a small-diameter back box and single-outlet tailpipe.

When new, all the JPS models had a black finish for the tailpipe, but few of these original tailpipes now survive because exhaust systems are consumables that get replaced regularly.

TRANSMISSION

The standard gearbox on all Mk II Capri models was a four-speed manual, but a three-speed automatic was an extra-cost option on all models except the Base 1300 and the 3.0 Ghia. On the Ghia it was standard, but on the Base 1300 it was not available at all.

Manual gearbox

With all 1.3-litre and 1.6-litre engines, the standard gearbox was a Ford Type 5. This has Reverse alongside First on the selector gate. However, the 2.0-litre and 3.0-litre cars retained the Granada gearbox used in Mk I models from late 1971. This is identifiable by three external operating rods, and by Reverse being located alongside Second on the gate.

The gear ratios were as shown below. Note that although the ratio sets in columns 2 and 3 are the same, the two gearboxes were of different types.

	1.3-litre & standard 1.6-litre	1600GT & 1.6 S	2000GT & 2.0 S	3000GT & 3.0 models
1	3.58:1	3.65:1	3.65:1	3.16:1
2	2.01:1	1.97:1	1.97:1	1.94:1
3	1.40:1	1.37:1	1.37:1	1.41:1
4	1.00:1	1.00:1	1.00:1	1.00:1
Rev	3.32:1	3.66:1	3.66:1	3.346:1

Clutch

The clutch on all manual-gearbox cars was a single dry plate type, but there were several different varieties.

On the British-built cars, the four-cylinder models all had Laycock clutches, with a 7.5in (190mm) diameter for 1.3 and standard 1.6 engines, but an 8.5in (216mm) diameter on the 1.6 GT and 2.0-litre engines. The 3.0-litre V6 cars built in Britain then had a Borg and Beck clutch with a 90.5in (242mm) diameter. The original clutch linings were by Mintex (H26) or Ferodo (2124F).

Cars built in Germany had locally-sourced clutches. The 1.3 and standard 1.6 engines had clutches made by LUK. For the 1.6 GT, clutches were dual-sourced, from LUK and from Fichtel & Sachs. For the 3.0-litre V6, all clutches came from Fichtel & Sachs. Linings were by Textar (50S/17) or Ferodo (2124F), with a third supplier of linings for the 3.0-litre in Mintex (H26). The German clutches had the same diameters as the British ones.

Automatic gearbox

The automatic gearbox option for the Capri Mk II was Ford's new C3 three-speed, a lightweight design that was manufactured at Bordeaux in France and made its first appearance in the US-market Pinto range of subcompacts. It became an extra-cost option on all variants of the Capri Mk II except for the base 1300 introduced in October 1975.

From April 1976, the automatic option was no longer available on S models, and at the same time it became standard on Ghia types. (Nevertheless, the manual gearbox remained available on Ghia models as an option.)

The gear ratios for the C3 automatic are 2.474:1, 1.474:1 and 1.000:1, with a Reverse ratio of 2.111:1.

Rear axle and final drive

The rear axle on all Mk II Capri models has a banjo casing that encloses a semi-floating hypoid final drive. However, there are two different types of axle. The lower-powered cars have a Timken Type J axle as standard, while the more powerful models have a Salisbury Type D axle, which looks physically stronger and has a longer differential nose-piece. There were also different ratios to suit different engines. Manual and automatic models shared the same final drive ratios.

The full list is as follows:

1.3-litre models	Timken type	4.125:1 final drive ratio
1.6-litre models	Timken type	3.778:1 final drive ratio
1.6 GT and S	Salisbury type	3.750:1 final drive ratio
2.0-litre models	Salisbury type	3.444:1 final drive ratio
3.0-litre models	Salisbury type	3.091:1 final drive ratio

Suspension

The Mk I Capri front suspension layout had proved successful and was carried over to the Mk II models. It consists of MacPherson struts with lower track-control arms and an anti-roll bar. The top of each strut is bolted through the inner wing and, as explained elsewhere, the inner wings on the 3.0-litre cars are specially reinforced.

The live rear axle is suspended on semi-elliptic springs, which are bolted and bushed directly to the bodyshell at the front but have swinging shackle mountings at the rear. Each spring has three leaves, but there are three different types of spring. The 1.3-litre and 1.6-litre cars share a standard type. The 2.0-litre and 3.0-litre cars have a second type, which also serves as the heavy-duty option for the two smaller-engined four-cylinder types. The third type is a heavy-duty option for the 2.0-litre cars, and no heavy-duty option was listed for the 3.0-litre models. Worth noting is that the spring rates on the Capri Mk II were considerably softer than those on the Mk I cars, reflecting Ford's intention to promote the newer model as more of a family car and less of a sporting machine.

Location for the rear axle is provided by an anti-roll bar. There is a single telescopic rear damper on either side of the axle, and all standard dampers were oil-filled types. However, gas dampers were used on the John Player Special models and with the X Pack.

STEERING AND BRAKES

All Mk II Capris were built with rack-and-pinion steering which has a 17.7:1 ratio. There was also a power-assisted rack with the same ratio, which was introduced in October 1975 as standard equipment on the 3.0-litre Ghia models. It later became standard on the S models as well, probably in October 1976, but the first S models did not have it. It was possible to have it deleted from the 3.0-litre models to special order, although probably only a few customers took advantage of that offer.

As on the Mk I Capri, the standard brakes were always solid discs at the front and drums at the rear. However, there were three different sizes of front disc, which were matched by three different sizes of rear drum brake. There was also a fourth type of front disc, a ventilated type associated with the X Pack. The different combinations are best explained in tabular form, as below:

	Front disc diameter	Rear drum dia & width
1.3-litre	9.5in	8 x 1.5in
1.6-litre & 2.0-litre	9.625in	9 x 1.75in
3.0-litre	9.7in	9 x 2.25in
X Pack	10.3in (ventilated)	9 x 2.25in

A vacuum servo was standard on all models.

WHEELS

There were five basic types of wheel for the Mk II Capri, all with a 13-inch diameter. Wheels for the lower-specification models were made of steel, but the more expensive and better-equipped models had alloys.

The silver-painted pressed-steel disc wheels used on entry-level Mk I Capris were carried over to the Mk II. They were characterised by ventilating cut-outs around the chromed hubcap, and had 4.5-inch rims.

The second type of wheel was a spoked steel sports type with a 5-inch rim, carried over from the last of the Mk I Capris and often described as the "dartboard" type. These

The plain disc wheels on entry-level models were the same as those on the final Mk I Capris. There was a row of perforations around the centre, and the securing nuts were concealed by a bright metal hubcap.

The early "sports" wheels were carried over from the last of the Mk I Capris. This one is on a 1977 1.6 L model. The blacked-out sections around the holes in the face helped to give the impression of a spoked wheel from a distance. These wheels are now usually known as 'dartboard' types.

CAPRI MK II WHEELS		
Base	Silver-painted pressed steel	
L	Silver-painted pressed steel	To September 1975
	Dartboard	From October 1975
GL	Dartboard	
GT	Silver-painted pressed steel	
	Dartboard	Extra-cost option
S	12-spoke Ronal alloy	
1.6 JPS	Four-spoke RS alloy with gold highlights	
2.0 Ghia	12-spoke Ronal alloy with black highlights	To September 1975
	12-spoke Ronal alloy	To September 1976
	Eight-spoke, plain finish	From October 1976
2.0 JPS	Four-spoke RS alloy with gold highlights	
3.0 Ghia	Eight-spoke, with black highlights and polished finish	To September 1975
	Eight-spoke, plain finish	From October 1975
3.0 JPS	Eight-spoke, with black and additional gold highlights	
Option	Four-spoke RS alloy	

These alloy wheels became standard on the S models during 1975.

Wider and more complex alloy wheels were standard wear on the Ghia models. The black highlights are tricky to restore and many owners have settled for wheels with an unpainted finish.

The wheels associated with the 3.0-litre Ghia were also used on the 3.0-litre John Player Special, but with the addition of gold highlights.

wheels have a silver-grey finish with either gloss or satin black on the outer sections of the recesses between the spokes. They also have a separate conical centre cap; on early cars this has a bright finish and a black centre, but on later ones it has a black finish with silver rings on the end face. Black securing nuts were standard. These wheels could also be had as an extra-cost option on models that did not have them.

A 12-spoke alloy wheel with a 5½-inch rim was the third type, and there were two different varieties of it. These wheels were made for Ford by Ronal, and carry both brand names cast into their faces. They have bright securing nuts and bright metal centre caps with black highlighting.

The Ronal wheels first appeared on the 1974-1975 2.0-litre Ghia models, when the sections between the spokes were painted black. The second version did not have the blacked-out sections, and was introduced for the Capri S in March 1975. It subsequently became standard wear on both the S models and the 2.0-litre Ghia, although it was replaced on the Ghia models after September 1976.

Then a fourth type of wheel was initially exclusive to the top-model 3.0-litre Ghia specification. These have 5½-inch rims and an eight-spoke design. Once again, they have bright metal securing nuts and bright metal centre caps. When new, these wheels had black highlighting and polished aluminium faces. A version with additional gold highlighting was used on the 3.0-litre versions of the John Player Special cars.

The fifth style of wheel was a four-spoke alloy type that is commonly known as the RS wheel and was an optional fit. Ford made this style of wheel over a number of years for several models in addition to the Capri, and there are multiple different types and sizes. There is still some controversy over which wheels were available for the Mk II Capris, but the overall consensus is that the correct ones have 7-inch rims and were made by Ronal; they carry Ronal identification on one spoke and RS identification on another, and use the flat-seat wheel nuts associated with the Mk II Capris. A version of this wheel with gold highlights was used on 1.6-litre and 2.0-litre versions of the John Player Special and associated all-black models.

There was also a deep-dish version of this wheel with a 7½-inch rim width that was made by ATS and was available only as part of the X Pack; these wheels carry ATS branding on one of the spokes. All varieties of the four-spoke RS wheel have a silver metallic finish and have push-in centre caps, usually with the RS logo.

It is worth noting that the 13-inch four-spoke wheels with 6-inch rims that were fitted to the Mk III Capri Laser models are not the same as those fitted to the Mk II cars. They have thicker spokes than the Mk II design and are made to suit taper-seat wheel nuts rather than the flat-seat nuts used on the Mk II models.

CAPRI MK II DETAILS

The "basic" dashboard with just two dials set in a veneered panel is seen here on a 1977 1.6 L model. The two-spoke steering wheel has a simple "Capri" logo in the centre, and there are three column stalks.

On base models, the instruments provided a bare minimum of information. Note the rectangular warning lights for the handbrake, oil pressure, lights and battery charging.

Tyres

The Mk II Capris were always supplied new with radial tyres, with the single exception of the Base 1300 model which had 6.00 x 13 cross-plies for its first year in production. The 1300 gained radials like the other cars in September 1976.

The standard tyres for other 1.3-litre models, and for the 1.6-litre and 2.0-litre, were 165SR13s. The 3.0-litre models had low-profile 185/70HR13 tyres, and these were available as an option on the 1600 GT and 2.0-litre models. They were also standard with the alloy wheels on the S models.

The 7½-inch wide wheels provided as part of the X Pack came with 205/60VR13 tyres as standard, and a 225/60VR13 size was optional.

DASHBOARD, INSTRUMENTS AND CONTROLS

The overall layout of the Mk II facia was carried over from the design that had proved so successful on the Mk I Capri. So the main element is a large instrument panel ahead of the driver, extending across the centre as well, and surrounded by crash padding that is usually upholstered with grained black

vinyl; on the 1974-1975 Ghia models only, the dashboard is trimmed to match the overall colour of the interior.

There is a drop-down glove box on the passenger's side which is lockable and has its own internal illumination, operated by a plunger switch on the outboard side. Both the glove box lid and the panel above it are trimmed in black vinyl to match that elsewhere on the dashboard. The upper panel is plain on most Mk II Capris, but on Ghia models it incorporates a grab handle. One of Ford's characteristic eyeball ventilators is fitted at each outboard end of the facia.

Dials and warning lights

As on the Mk I Capri, Ford created two major versions of the instrument panel. The "basic" version has two dials which are accompanied by rectangular warning lights, and the "sports" version has two main dials with four smaller satellite dials and round warning lights. Both versions have the radio, the heater controls, and some auxiliary switches in the centre of the car, roughly above the transmission tunnel and gear selector.

The basic two-dial dashboard was used on Base, L, XL and GL models. On Base, XL and 1975-season L models it would always have a black face panel; on the later L and the GL models it has a fake wood veneer face panel. The two major

The radio is an aftermarket item but is located in the standard position, above the heater control panel and the row of switches. One switch position has a blanking plate, and the heated rear window switch incorporates a warning light.

The "sports" dashboard is seen here on a 1975 Capri S. The face panel is trimmed in black vinyl and there are four satellite dials around the main pair. The warning lights are all round, and the three-spoke steering wheel carries crossed flags on its hub. There is just one column stalk, and the four switches along the lower dashboard rail are all visible.

CAPRI MK II DETAILS

The rev counter is on the inboard side in this RHD car. Note the yellow km/h markings on the speedometer, and the addition of a trip counter.

All the dials and warning lights have chromed bezels in this 3.0 Ghia model, and the steering wheel has Ghia identification on its hub. The radio is a period Ford type, fitting exactly into the cutouts in the panel. Also visible is the passenger's side grab handle associated with the Ghia models.

This is an original Ford-branded radio, in the 3.0-litre John Player Special car. There is yet another arrangement of switches and warning lights below it, in this case incorporating a red anti-theft alarm light.

dials are a 140mph speedometer and a combined-instruments dial with a temperature gauge at the top and a fuel gauge at the bottom. The speedometer is marked in miles and kilometres, in each case in white, and has a mileometer but no trip counter. The relative positions of the two main dials differs between RHD and LHD cars: the speedometer is always in the outboard position and the combined-instruments dial in the inboard position. There was no handbrake warning light fitted to the Base or L specification cars, but all the more expensive models did have one among the cluster of warning lights.

The sports dashboard was used on the GT, S and Ghia models. This has its face panel trimmed in black grained vinyl, and the two main dials are a speedometer and rev counter. The speedometer is again marked to 140mph, but the inner markings (km/h on most RHD cars) are in yellow and the mileometer is accompanied by a trip counter with a reset button in the face of the dial. The rev counter reads to 7000rpm and has white face markings. As on the basic dashboard, the speedometer is always on the outboard side of the instrument panel, with the rev counter on the inboard side. Although the rev counters for the four-cylinder and six-cylinder cars look the same, they are not interchangeable.

The sports dashboard is often called the "six-dial" type because of its four satellite dials plus two main dials. The satellite dials contain a battery condition indicator (top inboard), an oil pressure gauge (bottom inboard), a fuel gauge (top outboard) and an engine temperature gauge (lower outboard). The bezels for all six dials are black on the GT and S models, but are made of chromed plastic on the Ghia models. The dials themselves were carried over from the later Mk I Capris.

Switches

The switches were located in two main groups on the early (UK-built) cars, but there were changes from October 1976 when all production began to come from Germany. These changes were associated with the change to ISO-pattern

FACTORY-ORIGINAL Ford Capri MK II & MK III

The main lighting switches were on the lower dashboard rail on the better-equipped Capri Mk II models. Also visible on this John Player Special 3.0-litre is the control for the hazard warning lights.

The glovebox interior was made of plastic, and had its own automatic illumination operated by the plunger switch visible here.

column stalks and the standardisation of a rear wash-wipe system that occurred at the same time (see below).

On the early cars, there are switches on the lower dash rail. On the outboard side of the steering column, these are for the main lights, and on the inboard side they are for the front and rear wipers. All these switches disappeared from the later dashboards.

Both early and late dashboards have provision for a row of four switches below the heater control panel in the centre of the car. These positions are used differently from model to model, and depending on the equipment fitted to the car. Unused positions have a black plastic insert to blank them off. On the early cars, reading from left to right, the positions are for Front fog lights, Rear fog lights, Windscreen wash-wipe, and Heated rear window. On the later cars, the positions (again from left to right) are for Rear fog lights, Rear washer, Rear wiper, and Heated rear window.

The "six-dial" dashboard also has a rotary control for the panel light rheostat, mounted between the upper inboard satellite dial and the radio panel; the basic dashboard has no rheostat control. Both types of dashboard have a hazard warning lights switch, mounted on the outboard side and underneath the main dash panel. Just below this is the bonnet release catch.

Heater controls

The heater controls are mounted in a recessed panel that occupies the position above the four warning lights. There are two sliders, controlling temperature and air distribution respectively, and a third switch controls the fan speed.

Radio

A radio was an extra-cost option on entry-level models but a Ford-branded push-button type was standard on the GT, the S and the Ghia models. There was provision to fit it above the heater control panel, where three shaped cutouts on the first cars allowed for the knobs and central panel of radio. From autumn 1975, the three separate cutouts were changed to a single shaped aperture. If no radio was fitted, a black plastic blanking panel covered the cutouts or aperture.

From February 1977, a less expensive manually tuned radio (with tuning via one of the rotary knobs) became optional for the Base and L models. The idea here was presumably to tempt buyers of these cheaper models to add a radio, when the higher price of the push-button set would otherwise have deterred them.

Steering wheel, column and stalk controls

The steering wheel used on early Mk II Capri models was carried over from the last of the Mk I types, and has a two-spoke design. On Base, L, XL and GT models the wheel has a Capri logo on the recessed hub. Base and L models always had a black steering wheel, but the wheel was coloured to match the interior trim on all other models. On the Ghia models, the rim of the steering wheel is wrapped in leather, and the hub carries a Ghia logo. On the first Ghia models, and probably until September 1976, the steering wheel is colour-matched to the rest of the interior.

From October 1975, a much more attractive three-spoke "sports" steering wheel became standard on the S models and remained unique to them. This has a crossed chequered flag emblem on the hub.

The steering column is neatly concealed under a circular black plastic housing, and an outboard extension of this houses the key-operated ignition switch. There are also column-mounted control stalks, with different arrangements on early and late models.

On all early models, there is a single stalk on the right of the steering column which covers the operation of direction indicators, main and dipped beam, headlamp flasher, and horn. The later models, from October 1976, have three stalks,

This close-up shows the gear lever of a manual-gearbox car with the L specification. The gaiter is attached to the floor by a plastic frame, and there is a bright metal collar at the top which allows it to move up and down the gear lever. There is also a large gaiter for the handbrake lever, again secured by a plastic frame that is screwed to the floorpan. The handbrake grip is ribbed black plastic.

which conform to new ISO requirements of the time. One stalk is on the inboard side (the left on a RHD car) and two are on the outboard side. The inboard one operates the horn and the turn signals; the outboard pair are for the wipers and the main lighting.

Major controls

Manual gear levers all have a black ball-type grip on a bright metal stalk, with a black vinyl gaiter below. There is a bright metal ring at the top of the gaiter, which on basic models is secured through the carpet by a black plastic rim. On GT, S and Ghia types, the gaiter is secured to the centre console.

Automatics have a selector arrangement carried over from the final Mk I Capris. There is a straight gate marked PRND21 in a domed console, and a black T-handle selector on a bright metal stalk. The gate itself mounts directly to the transmission tunnel in a housing when no console is fitted, or to the console when the car has one.

The pull-up handbrake is mounted between the front seats and has a ribbed black plastic grip. On cars with a centre console, the handbrake emerges from the front of the stowage box housing and its black fabric gaiter is secured to that housing, but on cars without a console, the gaiter is attached to the transmission tunnel carpet.

The foot pedals all have black rubber pads with ribbing that runs from side to side. Unlike the Mk I Capris, there is no special pedal trim for the more sporty models.

INTERIOR TRIM

Map light

A map-reading lamp was Ford's idea of a sporty accessory, and so one was made available for the GT models as part of the Sports Custom Pack. The same map-reading lamp became part of the specification for the S models.

The lamp itself is mounted inside the passenger's side windscreen pillar. The lamp body, arm and pivots are all in bright metal, and the lamp can be swung out of the way when not in use. (However, it is doubtful whether it would pass more recent safety legislation about potentially dangerous protrusions inside the car!)

Centre console

Ford followed its usual policy for the Mk II Capri, fitting a centre console to the more sporty and up-market models but leaving the standard cars with just carpet to cover the transmission tunnel.

There were two types of centre console. A short type that was essentially a stylish oddments tray that also provides a surround for the gear selector was fitted to the XL, GL (from August 1976) and the S models. This console has a rectangular cut-out for a clock in its front edge, but a clock was actually fitted only to the GT and GL models; on the XL and S models, the space was filled with a blanking plate.

This is the short centre console again, in this case with the automatic gearbox selector in a John Player Special 3.0-litre car. The clock is just visible at the front end of the console, and in this case the steering wheel centre simply bears a generic Capri identification.

Map light in position on the passenger's side windscreen pillar.

The short centre console is seen here in a Capri S, and in this case the space for the clock is filled by a blanking panel.

The Ghia interior has the long centre console with cubby box at the rear, and the handbrake emerges from the front of the cubby box extension. The clock can be seen at the front end of the console panel. In this case, the car has an automatic gearbox, and the T-handle and gate can be seen.

This shows the arrangement of the automatic selector, in this case in a short-console car – the 3.0-litre John Player Special.

Pedals had ribbed rubber pads to give grip. These are in the automatic-gearbox 3.0-litre John Player Special car.

The Ghia models have a different console. Although the front section has the same design as the "short" console, with an oddments tray, a surround for the gear selector, and a clock aperture, the separate rear section rises up to make a stowage box between the seats, with a padded lid that doubles as a centre armrest. Ghia models unsurprisingly always had the clock as standard, too.

CAPRI MK II DETAILS

The standard type of door trim is seen here on a 1977 1.6 model. Note the black release handle and escutcheon. The speaker was not a standard accessory but was typical of the period, and has been fitted very neatly.

The Ghia style of door trim was quite different, with ribbed cloth in the centre section and a carpeted lower panel. The door handle and escutcheon were in bright metal on these models, too.

The door trim on the Capri S was the same as on lower-specification cars except for the bright metal release handle and escutcheon.

Door trims, door seals and rear side trims

Door trim panels, also known as door cards, all have the same overall pattern but there are several variations. The basic trim material is vinyl, in a colour to match the interior trim.

The style found on low-specification models is completely trimmed in vinyl, with plenty of fake stitching to suggest that it might actually be trimmed in leather. A long armrest that doubles as a door pull is a central feature. There is a scalloped central contrast panel, which is outlined by a chromed plastic trim strip and incorporates moulded horizontal "pleats". The door release handle and its escutcheon are black, but the window winder handle has a chromed arm with a black facing strip and a black grip. On the S models, the style is the same but the release handle and its escutcheon are chromed.

The door trim on the Ghia models follows the same overall layout but has a differently shaped contrast panel which is also recessed, to give the impression that the door is more thickly padded. The trim has a carpeted bottom section delineated by a bright metal strip. There is further bright metal to delineate the contrast panel, which is upholstered in

Yet another variation of door trim is seen here on a John Player Special 3.0-litre model. Everything is blacked out. Note also the remote control for the door mirror

ribbed cloth. The armrest is more rounded and more thickly padded than on the lower-specification trims, while the door handle and escutcheon are in bright metal and the window winder is the same as on other models. On Ghia models with a remote-control driver's door mirror, the toggle for the adjuster is mounted on the door trim towards the front and near the top.

The panelling of the front door trims was carried over to the rear side panels, complete with chromed plastic highlight strip. The ash tray in the panel is black plastic.

On the John Player Special editions, there is a special door trim with a perforated vinyl feature panel. This is the same on all three varieties – 1.6, 2.0 and 3.0.

Rear side trims

The trim panels alongside the rear seat are upholstered in vinyl to match the door cards, and the feature panel with its moulded pleats that begins on the door is carried over from the front as well, along with the chromed plastic highlight strip when one is fitted. Each rear side trim panel contains a swivelling ashtray in black plastic.

Headlining, sun visors and interior mirror

The headlining is always made of perforated vinyl, which was supposed to add a sporty feel to the passenger cabin. On most models, the headlining is off-white, but on the JPS models it is black.

The rear-view mirror is mounted to a plinth on the windscreen header rail. A plain mirror was standard on low-specification models but a dipping type was fitted to the XL and above.

Carpets and flooring

The carpet on the floor of the passenger compartment is a single section, cut and moulded to shape. This means that there are differences between the carpets for manual and automatic cars. All carpets have a plastic heel mat for the driver that is sewn to the relevant area. On all models except the Ghia, the carpet is a loop pile type. Ghia models always had a visually more attractive cut-pile carpet.

On the base, L and S models, carpets were invariably Black. Two additional colours (Chocolate and Medium Tan) were introduced for GL models and above in October 1975, and two more (Dark Orange and Green) for the L and GL models in October 1976, although the Dark Orange seems to have been very uncommon and it is questionable whether it ever existed.

Ford boasted that there was more sound insulation on the GL models and above from October 1975. This was achieved by adding small extra sections of insulating material at strategic points on the front bulkhead and floor, although the difference it made to noise levels inside the car appears to have been minimal.

This picture of the head lining in a 1977 car fitted with a sunroof shows a number of features. The winding handle for the sunroof is recessed into the head lining, and there is an interior light above the door aperture. The passenger's side grab handle attached to the cantrail is dark grey.

Pictured on a Capri S, this passenger grab handle has a more rounded shape than the type seen on the 1977 car, and also has bright metal trim plates.

There was always a join line across the lining of the sunroof. This is a John Player Special car and the headlining is black.

CAPRI MK II DETAILS

SEATS, UPHOLSTERY AND SEAT BELTS

Front seats

All Capri Mk II models have separate front seats with backrests that fold forwards to give access to the rear seat. A sliding lever on the outboard side of each backrest releases the lock and allows the backrest to tip forwards. There are several different types of front seat, each one associated with a different model or models and each one with its own type of upholstery, which is of course also used on the rear seats. To avoid confusion, the different types of front seat and associated upholstery are listed in the sidebar under the models in which they were used.

The mid-range front seats are represented here by those in a 1977 1.6 L. The bolsters are in vinyl but the wearing surfaces are in fabric with a stitching pattern that gives a pleated effect. The release lever for the seat back is in the outboard side of the seat.

Front seats both tipped forwards to give access to the rear seat. On the entry-level and mid-range types, the seat backs did not have map pockets. Also visible here is one of the stalk mountings for the front seat belts, which bolts to the transmission tunnel. The overmats on the floor here were not standard.

FRONT SEAT AND UPHOLSTERY TYPES

Base models
L models built before October 1975
These seats have non-reclining backrests and do not have head restraints. They are upholstered in vinyl with heat-formed flutes that run front to rear.

XL models
L models built from October 1975
These seats have no head restraints, but they do incorporate reclining backrests. The reclining mechanism is locked and released by a chromed lever on the outboard edge of each seat. They are upholstered with vinyl bolsters and cloth wearing surfaces in a colour that closely (but not perfectly) matches the vinyl; the four stitched pleats in the cloth run from front to rear. The backs of the seats are also upholstered in vinyl.

GL models
Like the XL seats that they effectively replaced, these seats have no head restraints but do have reclining backrests. The GL seats have the usual vinyl rear faces but the fabric on the backrest and cushions extends right to the edges of each seat. The fabric also incorporates flutes that run both fore-and-aft and from side to side.

GT models
The GT models have shaped bucket-type seats, with reclining backrests but once again without headrests. They have vinyl bolsters with fabric wearing surfaces in a colour to match the vinyl, but in this case the pleating in the fabric runs from side to side.

The rake of the front seat backs could be adjusted with the aid of this chromed lever.

John Player Special models
The first type of seat to have a head restraint was the one used on the John Player Special models in March 1975. These are bucket-type seats with a reclining backrest, and the headrest is a solid chunky item with stitching running up the front and top, and a plain panel at the rear. These seats have black vinyl bolsters and head restraints, and contrasting gold fabric wearing surfaces in a cloth that Ford called Rialto. This cloth has been unavailable for some time.

S models
Headrests arrived on mainstream production Capris with the S models in October 1975. These seats again have reclining backrests and the headrests are thinner than those on the JPS cars, with two rows of stitching visible on the front face. The upholstery consists of black vinyl bolsters, wider than the JPS type, with cloth wearing surfaces in a contrasting colour: the contrast fabric was initially Rialto cloth that runs over the top of the seat back, but from March 1977 it changed to a boldly striped cloth called Cadiz. These "sports" seats could be ordered at extra cost on the less expensive models as well.

Ghia models
At the top of the range, the Ghia front seats have reclining backrests that incorporate built-in head restraint bolsters. On most Mk II Capri Ghia models, they also have vinyl bolsters with Rialto fabric wearing surfaces, but in this case the fabric extends to cover part of the bolster on each side of the cushion; this helps to give the impression that the seats are wrap-around bucket types – which they are not. The head restraint section is always trimmed in vinyl. From October 1977 the pleating pattern of the fabric section changed, to incorporate flutes that run both fore-and-aft and from side to side, similar to but not the same as the style used on the GL models.

45

These are the front seats on a 3.0 Ghia model. Fabric covers the whole of the cushion's upper surface, and also wraps across the side sections of the backrests. There is also a fixed head restraint section, upholstered in vinyl.

With the seat tipped forwards, it is clear how the rear of the Ghia type differs from the seats in the mid-range cars. The built-in head restraint is obvious, as is the map pocket.

The rear seat was resolutely designed for two people only. This is the mid-range type.

These are the special front seats in a Capri S. They have separate, adjustable head restraints, and the wearing surfaces are upholstered with "gold" cloth, as had been done with the John Player Special cars.

The head restraints in the rear seats of Ghia models were rather more of a token effort than those on the front seats. The fabric facings for the cushions again covers their full width and makes them appear wider and more luxurious than the standard type.

Rear seats

The rear seat back was designed to fold forwards to give the extended load space that customers expected with the hatchback configuration of the Capri Mk II. There were two different varieties. A one-piece seat back was used on the early (1975-model) L specification cars and on the Base models that followed them for the 1976 and later model-years. However, on all the more expensive models, the seat back was divided into two independently foldable sections, an arrangement that allowed greater versatility of the loadspace. From October 1975, the split backrest was also made standard on the L models.

CAPRI MK II DETAILS

The upholstery of the Capri S is seen again on the rear seats. It is easy to see why this upholstery did not wear well. In this case, there was no pretence at head restraints.

The gold upholstery is seen again here in a John Player Special model. This is a 3.0-litre car, and therefore has the style of seating associated with the V6 models. The driver's side headrest is actually mounted back to front in this case, perhaps to give the driver greater comfort.

The upholstery style reserved for the top-model 3.0-litre cars was of course continued on the rear seats as well. This combination of colour and style could perhaps only have been dreamed up in the 1970s!

The original safety belts carried tags like this, bearing both the Ford logo and the name of their manufacturer.

Seat belts

Seat belts were always standard for the front seats, but those for the rear seats were always an extra-cost option and remained rare as a result.

The standard belts that Ford fitted were always inertia-reel types designed for one-handed operation, and those for the front seats had black plastic receivers on stalks that were bolted to the sides of the transmission tunnel. They were manufactured on Ford's behalf by Wingard, and when new carried identification labels. However, many cars have by now been fitted with replacement belts after the old ones have become unserviceable.

Boot interior

The boot area has moulded plastic side panels, which also cover the inner rear wheelarches. These came in Black, Brown or Beige to suit the interior trim – but it is not unknown for cars to be fitted with a non-matching colour, which was another instance of using what was available to keep the assembly lines moving. These side panels have hook clips around their top edges to suit the hanging straps attached to the optional loadspace cover.

Some models have an automatically-operated boot light, with a plunger switch that is actuated by the opening or closure of the hatchback. There were always two on the Ghia models and on the GT, but on the GL and S models Ford economised by fitting only one, which was on the left-

This was the standard arrangement for the boot in the mid-range models. There are moulded black side panels to protect and conceal the metalwork of the inner wings and wheelarches, and the hook clips for the loadspace cover are mounted to these. The floor is carpeted.

The loadspace cover is seen in place here.

The loadspace cover folded up and could be stowed in the boot, in the black vinyl pouch seen here. The rear seats have both been folded forwards in this picture, although they could of course be folded individually if required. Note that they did not provide a completely flat loading floor: there is a distinct step between the boot floor and the folded seat backs.

Boot arrangements in the Ghia models were slightly different. The most obvious feature here is the protective strips running across the carpet and up the rear seat backs. There is also a boot light in the side panel above the left-hand rear wheelarch.

hand side. These lights are mounted in the plastic wheelarch protection panels.

There are three types of boot floor covering. The most basic is a simple black rubber mat, which is found on the 1300 models that were introduced in October 1975. All the mid-range models have a simple loop pile carpet which is cut to shape, and is invariably in black. On the Ghia models, there is cut-pile carpet with rubber-faced metal protective strips that are attached through the carpet and run from front to rear.

These are matched by short lengths of the same protective strip on the carpeted backs of the rear seats.

Rear loadspace cover

A rear loadspace cover was an extra-cost option for all models except Ghia types, where it was standard. Sometimes rather grandly described as a rear parcels shelf (which it certainly was not), it was simply a vinyl-trimmed flexible panel that could be located on hooks around the top of the boot area. On cars built in the first year of production, there were also female press-studs that engaged with their male counterparts on the backs of the rear seats.

The value of this loadspace cover was in concealing the contents of the boot, which could otherwise be clearly seen

CAPRI MK II DETAILS

A full set of original handbooks is a desirable accompaniment to any Capri. This set belongs to the 3.0-litre John Player Special.

With the boot floor removed, the spare wheel, rear washer reservoir and pump, and tool kit are all exposed. Note how the spare wheel is secured in place by a single bolt. The rubber bellows on the right is for the fuel filler neck that leads to the underfloor tank on the right.

from outside through the hatchback window. However, it was never a very convincing piece of equipment, and even less so after October 1975 when the press-studs were deleted. Owners tended not to use it, and often simply threw it away. When not in use, the cover could be folded up and stored inside a plastic pouch, which tended to go the same way as the cover itself.

Spare wheel well and tools

The whole boot floor can be lifted out to give access to the items below. The spare wheel is carried here, lying flat in a recess that is offset to the left. To the left of the spare wheel and at the rear of the car is a translucent plastic reservoir for the rear window washer, and the washer pump is located on the same side but in front of the wheel.

The screw-type jack is located to the right rear of the wheel, along with a wheel nut wrench. These were normally painted either blue or black, but for the all-black John Player Special models, Ford seem to have taken care to provide a black one.

MK II INTO MK III

It has been claimed that Ford Motorsport issued kits to convert a Mk II into a Mk III lookalike in the late 1970s. These were for racing customers, and were correspondingly rare. They consisted of a front end and bonnet panels, headlamps and a spoiler.

THE X PACK

Strictly speaking, the X Pack was known to Ford as the Series X. It was launched near the end of Capri Mk II production in August 1977 and was a collection of performance and handling upgrades for the 3.0 S model, although there were also optional items that could be added to any smaller-engined Capri to give it a high-performance look. Series X upgrades were available only through Ford RS dealerships, and there were comparable upgrades for Fiesta, Escort and Cortina models as well. The X Pack for the Capri remained available until 1980, well past the end of Capri Mk II production, and could also be had for the Mk III models (see p105).

The full package of Series X upgrades for a 3000 S added £2331 to the standard car's £7294, but buyers could select what they wanted from the options available on top of the basic package. The X Pack kits drew on parts sourced from Ford Of Britain, Ford AVO, and German tuner Zakspeed, who had been running Capris in the European racing series.

The basic Series X modifications lifted power of the 3.0-litre engine to 175bhp and torque to 194 lb ft, which delivered 130mph and a 0-60 acceleration time of 7.4 seconds. The engine changes consisted of triple Weber carburettors, bigger inlet and exhaust valves, and cast alloy manifolds, plus an electric fuel pump.

On top of that came the Series X options. Handling could be improved by stiffened suspension, with an uprated front anti-roll bar and an anti-dive kit. A limited-slip differential was available, as were 10.3in ventilated front disc brakes with calipers from the Ford Granada. The rear brakes were the 9in x 2.25in drums otherwise standard on 3.0-litre models. Further options were four-spoke alloy wheels with 7½in rims, and these could be fitted with either 205/60 or 225/60 tyres. To cover these, there was a Zakspeed bodykit made from GRP and consisting of four wide "Spa" wheelarch extensions, plus matching front and rear spoilers. The right-hand rear wheelarch extension incorporated a new fuel filler flap, and the front spoiler contained brake cooling ducts.

THE JOHN PLAYER SPECIAL LIMITED EDITION

Ford's involvement with Formula 1 racing through the Lotus team that was sponsored by cigarette maker John Player provided the theme for the only special-edition Capri Mk II. This was introduced in March 1975 at the Geneva Motor Show, and was built only at Halewood; production ended in June, just as the cars began to reach Ford showrooms.

The name has been a source of some confusion; Ford actually called it a Capri S and intended it to be an early preview of the S models that would replace the GT types later in the year. However, when *Autocar* magazine tried a pre-production example in June 1975, it described the car as a 2000S GT (and also managed to describe its Pinto engine as a Kent type).

A total of 2003 cars is believed to have been built, and most of them featured the distinctive black and gold livery of the Lotus John Player Special racing cars. As a result, they are generally known as the John Player Special edition or JPS. In some countries outside the UK, these cars were known as Midnight or Blackbird editions when new, although enthusiasts today normally refer to them as JPS types. An unknown quantity – sometimes claimed to be as large as 25% of the total built – had white paintwork rather than the black usually associated with them. The black paint was known as Ebony Black, although it is sometimes called Midnight Black.

The base model for this all-black edition was normally a 1.6 GT, but the JPS was also available as a 2.0 GT or a 3.0 GT and probably the majority of those sold in the UK had one of the larger engines. Although stiffer suspension with gas dampers was part of the package, that was the only non-standard mechanical feature and the emphasis was firmly on appearance. All models of the Capri S had alloy wheels, those wheels having different designs according to the engine size fitted. On the 1.6-litre and 2.0-litre cars, the wheels were four-spoke RS alloys with the centre of each spoke finished in gold paint, and on the 3.0-litre models they were a version of the wheel used on the 3.0 Ghia, again with gold highlights.

Both black and white examples of the Capri S had blacked-out brightwork, and the black examples had black bumpers as well. All of them also carried a very distinctive decal striping kit in gold, which in conjunction with the black paint option mimicked the John Player Special Formula 1 racing livery. (Note that the similar treatment introduced on the volume-production S models was not exactly the same; only on the JPS cars did the gold decals continue across the rear of the car, and there were other differences as well.)

The Capri S had an engine size badge in gold on each front wing in what would become the standard position when the volume-production S model replaced the GT later in the year. The cars finished in white also had the gold striping, but they combined blacked-out brightwork with white bumpers.

Both black and white cars retained the black theme for the interior, which had a black headlining and black vinyl seat bolsters with gold cloth inserts for the wearing surfaces. The interior brightwork was also black, with an epoxy powder coating. Carpets remained black. Some cars were of course supplied with extra-cost options such as a radio, tinted glass, a laminated windscreen and a sunroof, none of which Ford saw fit to make standard on these special-edition models.

The John Player Special cars were very distinctive indeed, with gold lining and gold highlights on their wheels. This is a 3.0-litre model, with the twin tailpipes characteristic of the type and, of course, "3.0" badges on the wings.

The gold striping extended to cover the frame of the radiator grille – something not duplicated on the striped S models released later the same year.

In this picture, it is clear how the twin side stripes slim down to a single stripe running across the rear panel at top and bottom.

CAPRI MK II DETAILS

FORD CAPRI MK III, 1978-1986

Top model of the early Mk III Capri range was once again a 3.0-litre V6 with the Ghia trim. This 1981 model belongs to Charles Newman and is finished in metallic Crystal Green.

Even though sales figures had been on a downward trajectory throughout the life of the Capri Mk II, Ford considered that there was still enough interest in the range to justify keeping it in production for a few more years. So the Capri was given a limited-budget but very effective facelift, emerging in March 1978 as the Capri Mk III.

Production for the UK was once again confined exclusively to the German factory at Cologne – although a few cars were also built at Saarlouis before presses and patterns were consolidated at Cologne. Then, no doubt confounding the expectations of doubters both inside and outside the company, Capri production continued for a further nine years until it was brought to a close at the end of 1986.

The year before the Capri Mk III's introduction, 1977, marked a watershed in Capri history because it was also the first year when global sales dipped below 100,000 cars. The arrival of the new model did have a positive effect, though, and sales bounced back up again in 1978 and further still in 1979 as the new Mk IIIs attracted buyers. However, it was obvious that the golden age of the Capri was now over. Mk III production peaked at 85,420 in 1979 and more than halved the following year. After that, there was a gradual downward slide until the end in 1986, and for its final two years the Capri was built only with right-hand-drive and predominantly for buyers in Britain.

Ford had been working on a facelift for the Capri as early as the 1976 Geneva Show, when they displayed a Mk II model with a front end similar to that of the Escort RS2000 and with a rear spoiler. The facelift went ahead as Project Carla, and the facelifted cars were eventually introduced at the Geneva Show in March 1978. Although Ford always saw them as simple facelifts of the second-generation Capri, the public soon began to call them Capri Mk III models. The DVLA in Britain nevertheless took a little time to catch up, and many cars built in 1978 were shown on the V5 registration document as Mk II models – correctly, as far as Ford were concerned.

The changes, overseen by Ford of Europe's design chief, Uwe Bahnsen, were much less far-reaching than the popular new name would suggest. However, Ford had done a very good job of making the cars look new and different. Rejecting the design shown at Geneva in 1976, they had redesigned the front end with twin round headlamps and a slightly longer bonnet that gave a "brow" over them; there were new wraparound bumpers, and redesigned, ribbed tail light units. Then there was a chin spoiler as standard, which was accompanied on the S models by a tail spoiler as well. These certainly made the cars look more sporty than before, although Ford claimed that they were primarily intended to reduce fuel consumption and improve the Capri's susceptibility to side winds. Perhaps they were, although they were not very successful at the latter!

There were other, smaller cosmetic changes. On the mechanical side, the five launch engines were all carried over from the Mk II models. They consisted of the 1.3-litre OHV, 1.6-litre, 1.6-litre GT and 2.0-litre OHC Pinto, and 3.0-litre V6. These were accompanied by just five trim specifications, called Base, L, GL, S and Ghia. From these elements, Ford created a ten-model UK range of 1300 (always called that despite its "1.3" badges) and 1.3 L, 1.6 L and 1.6 GL, 1.6 S, 2.0 GL, 2.0 S and 2.0 Ghia, and 3.0S and 3.0 Ghia.

This full range did not last for long, and in fact the entry-level 1300 model was withdrawn before the end of 1978, making it one of the rarest of the Mk III models in Britain. Although the other nine models would remain available until the major watershed for the range in the summer of 1981, the public's enthusiasm for the Capri Mk III was already beginning to decline during 1979 and Ford recognised the need to support sales in some way. Their choice was to focus on limited-edition models, introduced at strategic times and at strategic price points as required. These models offered buyers a degree of exclusivity but did not cost a lot extra to build. So the first one was introduced during March 1980 in Britain, as the Capri GT4, which was intended to boost sales in the middle of the Capri range.

The summer 1981 watershed was actually preceded by three more limited editions, which of course helped to draw attention to the range and created a halo of excitement that added to the impact of the revised mainstream models. These three limited editions were the Capri Cameo (at the bottom end of the range), the Capri Tempo, and the Capri Calypso, the last being a mid-range model that introduced eye-catching two-tone paintwork to the Capri Mk III.

The major change in summer 1981 was that the by now elderly British-built 3.0-litre "Essex" V6 engine was withdrawn and in its place came a German-built 2.8-litre V6. This had a much more modern design and was known as the "Cologne" engine after its place of origin. It also introduced fuel injection to the Capri range, and this accounted for the "2.8i" name that was commonly used, although the cars were correctly known as 2.8 Injection models. Unsurprisingly, it

Capri marketing was heavily supported by special-edition models, and Ford came up with a range of attractive special features for the Calypso edition in summer 1981. Based on a mid-range 1.6 LS, it always had two-colour paintwork, like this example owned by Terry Garnett. The two colours are Medium Blue Metallic and Silver Metallic.

FACTORY-ORIGINAL FORD CAPRI MK II & MK III

From October 1984, the mainstream specification for 1.6-litre and 2.0-litre models went by the name of Laser. This 1985 car is owned by Margaret Elliott and is finished in Strato Silver.

gave the Capri a new lease of life in performance terms, and the halo effect of this new top model must certainly have helped sales of the lesser Capris over the next few years.

Meanwhile, there were also some changes lower down the range, which was quite drastically slimmed down in the process. Like its British-built 3.0-litre cousin, the British-built 1.3-litre engine went out of production – but in this case it was not replaced. So the range now began with 1.6 L and 1.6 GL models. Out went the old 1.6 S, partly to give the new Ford XR3 sporty hatchback a clear run at that sector of the market, and in its place came the new 1.6 LS model – really a 1.6 L with some elements of the S specification added.

The S specification remained available with the 2.0-litre engine, but that engine could not now be had with any other level of trim. Then at the top of the range came the new 2.8i. So for the 1982 season, the Capri Mk III range in the UK consisted of just five models – half as many as when the Mk III had been introduced in 1978. These were the 1.6 L, 1.6 GL, 1.6 LS, 2.0 S, and 2.8i.

This pruned range was more appropriate to the level of Capri sales, which was still on the decline. But well-executed limited editions were still needed from time to time. So in May 1982 the Capri Cabaret (in both 1.6-litre and 2.0-litre forms) boosted sales of the mid-range models, and a Capri Calypso

II followed up on the success of the 1981 two-tone special edition. A second version of the Cabaret – imaginatively called the Cabaret II – gave 1.6-litre and 2.0-litre sales a boost in January 1983. At about the same time, five-speed manual gearboxes became available for the 2.8 and 2.0 models, although it was by this stage too late for them to have very much of an effect on sales.

So from March 1983 the Capri range was reduced once again, this time from five models down to three. The two lower levels of trim, L and GL, disappeared altogether and the lowest-priced Capris were now the models that had earlier been the core of the range – the 1.6 LS and 2.0 S. Above them the 2.8 Injection was still the top option.

This three-model range – boosted from September 1983 by the legendary Tickford Turbo, an officially sanctioned, aftermarket high-performance derivative – lasted until September 1984. At that point, the LS and S trim options were rationalised to a single type, which was known as Laser. In fact, the Laser had been introduced in June 1984, when it was described as a limited edition positioned between the LS and S models. This was a clever piece of marketing that undoubtedly helped to give the impression that the mainstream Laser models from October 1984 (which were no different from the earlier ones) were also limited editions – but of course they were not. Meanwhile, the V6 model was rebranded as a 2.8 Injection Special, which certainly made it sound exciting even though the actual changes to it were mostly cosmetic. In Germany, it was sold with the name of 2.8 Super Injection from April 1984, but there were relatively few of these, because left-hand-drive Capri production came to an end over the summer of 1984.

The Laser models were greatly enhanced by four-spoke alloy wheels and a rear spoiler as standard. This is again the 1985 2.0-litre model in Strato Silver.

FACTORY-ORIGINAL FORD CAPRI MK II & MK III

The Tickford Turbo created its own legend, and was a semi-official Ford "special" that was actually hand-built by Aston Martin Tickford and was formidably expensive. This example belongs to Jon Cristini.

As Capri production drew to a close in December 1986, Ford had one more marketing trick up its sleeve. The final 2.8-litre models were turned into a special edition (there were too many of them for it to be a limited edition) that was called the Capri 280 and had a selection of special equipment. These cars did not go on sale in Britain until March 1987, and acquired the unofficial name of Brooklands, after their special green paintwork. Ford had originally intended to build 500 examples and to call this edition the Capri 500, but there was strong demand in the beginning, and a total of 1038 examples was eventually built. That demand nevertheless seems to have been driven by the dealers, and in practice the Capri 280 was a slow seller, even though it has since become a sought-after variant of the car. High cost was probably a deterrent to sales when the cars were new, and the final examples were not sold until 1989.

Although Ford never really replaced the Capri, they did revive its name in 1988 for an Australian-built 2+2 convertible that was based on the floorpan of the Mazda 323. Although this sold quite well and a version was shipped to the USA as the Mercury Capri, the model never came to Europe before it went out of production in 1994. It was a good car in its own right, but it was not a Capri in the mould of the classic European Ford coupés that had been built between 1968 and 1986.

Today, the later Mk III models, and especially those with the 2.8-litre V6 engine, are very much sought after by Capri enthusiasts.

In 1986, the final run of cars were 2.8-litre models with a number of special features that were known as Capri 280 or Brooklands types. This one is owned by Mark Smith, who is Registrar of the Ford Capri 280 Register.

THE GERMAN MK III CAPRIS

The German Mk III range introduced in March 1978 consisted of 11 models. These were the 1.3 L and 1.3 GL, 1.6 L and 1.6 GL, 1.6 S, 2.0 with Pinto or V6 engines, 2300 S and 2300 Ghia with German V6 engines and the 3.0S and 3.0 Ghia with Essex V6 engines. From April 1979, the 2.3-litre V6 was uprated from 108bhp to 114bhp, but in other respects the German range developed in the same way as its UK counterpart; the cars were after all now being built in the same factory.

July 1981 then brought the very special Zakspeed Turbo model, which was sold on the back of the Zakspeed Capris' success in German touring car racing. These cars had a 2.8-litre Cologne V6 engine with KKK turbocharger, a large front air dam and rear spoiler, plus wider wheelarches. Around 200 were built.

Production of LHD Capris ended in November 1984, and thereafter all Capris assembled at Cologne were RHD types predominantly for the UK market.

The German-built "Cologne" 2.8-litre V6 engine took over from the British-built 3.0-litre V6 from 1981. This Ford publicity picture shows an early car with the new engine – prominently badged as a Capri 2.8 Injection.

A QUICK OVERVIEW

The complexity of the Mk III range is hard to grasp, so this simplified table is designed to help.

1300	1978 only	1.3-litre
L	1978-1982	1.3-litre or 1.6-litre
GL	1978-1982	1.6-litre or 2.0-litre
S	1978-1984	1.6-litre (1978-1980)
		2.0-litre (1978-1984)
		3.0-litre (1978-1981)
Ghia	1978-1982	2.0-litre (1978-1982)
		3.0-litre (1978-1981)
LS	1981-1984	1.6-litre
2.8 Injection	1981-1984	2.8-litre
Tickford Turbo	1983-1986	2.8-litre turbo
2.8 Injection Special	1984-1986	2.8-litre
Laser	1984-1986	1.6-litre or 2.0-litre

For details of the special edition models, please see p102.

The Mk III Capri was just as popular with British police forces as its Mk II predecessor. This one was owned by the Hampshire Police and is a 1979 3.0 S model. To lower the car's profile, it was ordered in a standard Ford colour and the side decals of the S specification models were not fitted. (PVEC)

WEIGHTS AND MEASURES

Wheelbase	100.9in (2563mm)	
Front track	53.3in (1353mm)	
Rear track	54.5in (1384mm)	
Length	172.3in (4376mm)	
Width	66.9in (1698mm)	
Height	52.1in (1323mm)	
Wheels	13-inch steel disc with 5-inch rim	
	13-inch steel with 5.5-inch rim	
	13-inch alloy with 5.5-inch rim	
	13-inch alloy with 6-inch rim	
	13-inch alloy with 7-inch rim	
	13-inch alloy with 7.5-inch rim (X-Pack)	
	13-inch RS alloy with 7-inch rim	
	15-inch RS alloy with 7-inch rim	
Tyres	165 SR 13 radial	
	185/70 SR 13 radial	
	185/70 HR 13 radial	
	205/60 x 13 radial	
	225/60 x 13 radial (X Pack option)	
	195/50 x 15 radial	
Unladen weight	1.3	2227 lb (1010kg)
	1.6	2293 lb (1040kg)
	1.6 S	2326 lb (1055kg)
	2.0	2194 lb (995kg)
	2.8i	2712 lb (1230kg)
	3.0 Ghia	2580 lb (1170kg)
	Tickford	2745 lb (1245kg)
0-60mph	1.3	20 sec (19.5 sec from 1979)
	1.6	13.5 sec
	1.6 S	12.5 sec manual; 16.0 sec automatic (12.0 sec and 15.0 sec from late 1979)
	2.0	10.8 sec
	2.8i	7.8 sec
	3.0	8.5 sec manual; 10.0 sec automatic
	3.0 X-Pack	7.4 sec
Max speed	1.3	89mph (143km/h) 91mph (146km/h from 1979)
	1.6	98mph (157km/h)
	1.6 S	106mph (170km/h) (109mph/175km/h from late 1979)
	2.0	111mph (179 km/h)
	2.8i	130mph (210km/h)
	3.0	122mph (196km/h) manual; 118mph (190 km/h) automatic
	3.0 X-Pack	130mph (209km/h)

More conventionally marked, this 1983 Capri belonged to the Greater Manchester Police. It was a 2.8-litre V6 model. Note the auxiliary lights hanging below the bumper and the blue "police" lights located ahead of the grille.

This late 2.8-litre car was also operated by the Greater Manchester Police, and became the last Capri to remain in service with that force. In this case, no auxiliary lights were fitted. (PVEC)

PRODUCTION FIGURES

Note that these figures are for total Capri Mk III production and do not show the numbers of Capri Mk III models sold in the UK market. (It is currently impossible to provide a reliable figure for this, and Ford have always been vague about it.) They are best used as a guide to the overall trends and to the relative popularity of each of the models listed. However, the figures for 1985 and 1986 are a reasonably accurate guide to UK sales, as production in Germany during those years was only of RHD models, most of which were for the UK.

German-made Capri types that were not available in the UK are not listed here, and overall totals would therefore be meaningless. The 1978 figures inevitably include some of the last Capri Mk II models.

	1300	1600	2000	2.8i	3000
1978	3070	25,248	26,412		4916
1979	3246	36.329	31,345		7966
1980	1348	19,032	16,228		2131
1981	582	16,162	9567	5747	931
1982		12,659	7650	4091	
1983		11,483	8793	5767	
1984		7709	5818	4615	
1985		4373	3175	1714	
1986		4608	3444	2658	

UK Capri sales for the Capri's final years, as quoted by Chris Rees (in *Essential Ford Capri*) were 22,254 in 1983, 16,328 in 1984, and 11,075 in 1985.

CAPRI MK III DETAILS

Just as with the Mk II Capris, it is only possible to provide details of the specification that Ford intended to use on these cars. Rather than hold up the assembly lines because of a shortage of the correct (non-critical) parts, it was standard practice at Ford's German plants to use whatever fitted as long as there were adequate supplies to hand. As a result there are some cars with what are best considered as "non-standard" specifications. Ford enthusiasts have learned to live with such things.

BODYSHELL AND PANELS

Front valance panel

The steel front valance panel of the Mk III Capris is quite different from the Mk II equivalent because it incorporates a chin spoiler. This was a fundamental element in the improved aerodynamics of the Mk III cars, and was used on all varieties, from the humblest 1300 right up to the 2.8 Injection.

All front valances had four small holes when they were new. These were for mounting the optional – but uncommon – auxiliary lights.

Bonnet slam panel

The bonnet slam panel has the same configuration as the Mk II type; that is, there is a receiver for the bonnet catch in the centre, and the triangular support bracket for the bonnet prop rod is pressed out of the slam panel at the left-hand end. The prop rod itself is black passive coated, and has a retaining washer at the slam panel end; the end of the rod is flattened to retain it in place. Again as on the Mk II cars, the prop rod on earlier Mk IIIs is stowed in position across the top of the slam panel. On cars built before autumn 1982, it is located when stowed by a four-pronged white plastic receiver clip on the right-hand side – unless, of course, that has been broken and replaced by a non-original clip. On later models, a black clip with two angled prongs was fitted at the factory.

Once again like the Mk II, the spring for the bonnet catch is mounted above the slam panel just ahead of the receiver, and is not painted because it was installed after the bodyshell had been painted.

A pressed metal panel is bolted to the slam panel and runs back to the radiator. This is designed to funnel air from the grille through the radiator and there are different types with different engines. On four-cylinder cars, the pyramidal pressings within each "frame" of the panel are shallow. On 3.0-litre cars, the pyramidal shape is more defined, and on the 2.8-litre cars there is a shorter panel to suit the different radiator; again, the pyramidal pressings are well-defined. On very late cars, built from October 1986, there are four rivets visible in the air duct panel. These hold the relays for the dim-dip headlights that were fitted from that date.

The car's identification plate is riveted to the left-hand side of the slam panel (as viewed from in front of the car), and in the corresponding position on the right is the build plate. This normally shows the engine number and build date, the trim code, and the original paint code, sometimes with the paint name as well. The build plate was often attached to the shell (by two equal-sized rivets) before it went through the paint shop and is therefore painted to match the body; however, on several cars the plate retained a primer finish and was therefore clearly not in place when the shell passed through the paint shop. There is so far no explanation for these anomalies.

This view of the slam panel on a 1986 Laser model confirms that the spring for the bonnet catch, and its associated fixing tag, were not painted in the body colour.

CAPRI MK III DETAILS

The lightly pyramidal shape of the air duct pressings on a four-cylinder car are clear in this picture.

This late Laser model displays the four rivets in the air duct associated with the dim-dip headlight system.

Front inner wings

Again as on the Mk II Capris, there are different front inner wings for the four-cylinder and V6 cars. The essential shape of the inner wings is always the same, but on the V6 models, both 3.0-litre and 2.8-litre types, there are pressed steel reinforcing plates welded around the tops of the suspension struts and extending down the inner face of the wing. The inside area of the inner wing also has reinforcing plates that are extended to run along the bottom edge. The wings on the six-cylinder cars are also braced to the bulkhead by a triangular plate on each side.

All inner wings were already in place when the bodyshells passed through the paint shop, and are therefore painted to match the rest of the bodyshell. Nonetheless, towards the end of the production run there is no doubt that Ford had started to skimp on paint, and some late cars seem to have had only the thinnest of coatings on the inner wings – so they have often rusted badly.

There is a triangular panel at the front of each inner wing, concealing and protecting a cut-out that gives access to the rear of each headlamp unit. These panels are always made of black plastic. In the beginning they were simply clipped in place, but these early covers tended to come loose and fall into the engine bay. So a single screw was later added to each one to secure it to the top of the inner wing. Just in front of each of these cover panels is an adjustable bonnet buffer with a round black rubber head.

On the top surface of the left-hand inner wing (as seen from the front of the car) is a sticker that contains advice about anti-freeze in several languages. On earlier Mk III Capris, this sticker has a white background, but from 1981 its background is yellow. This sticker is always arranged so that it can be

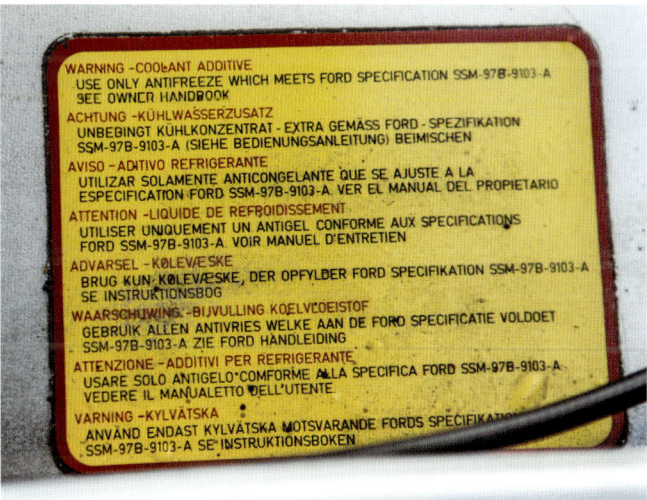

This yellow sticker was attached to the inner wing to give guidance on using anti-freeze.

On the 2.8-litre V6 models, the injection pump was mounted low down by the left-hand front wing and there was a rubber pad on the inner wing to prevent chafing of the fuel lines. Note the yellow coolant sticker here, which is on the opposite inner wing on all models except the 2.8 V6 types.

FACTORY-ORIGINAL FORD CAPRI MK II & MK III

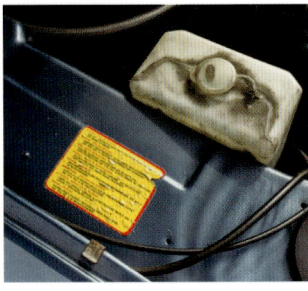

The position of the coolant sticker could vary quite a lot. In this case (the car is a Calypso special edition), it is much further away from the edge of the inner wing than on the 1985 Laser illustrated on page 61.

The reinforcing plates over the front strut mountings are clear in this picture of a 3.0-litre Ghia model.

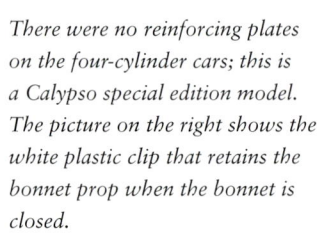

There were no reinforcing plates on the four-cylinder cars; this is a Calypso special edition model. The picture on the right shows the white plastic clip that retains the bonnet prop when the bonnet is closed.

Later models had an angled clip for the bonnet prop rod, with just two prongs.

read by somebody standing at the side of the car. However, its precise position on the inner wing can vary by several inches, and on the 2.8-litre V6 models it is actually on the opposite inner wing because of the relocated battery.

Also on the left-hand inner wing (as seen from the front) of cars built from 1979 is a warning notice about the asbestos used in braking components. Original stickers always have a portrait format; the landscape type sometimes seen on restored cars was used on later Ford models but not on the Capri.

Bulkhead

The later Mk III bulkheads were not painted on the engine side. The early ones were painted, and the very early ones (from April to November 1978) had the same sound deadening material as the Mk II cars. However, the later cars had neither paint nor sound deadening. It is not clear exactly when this change occurred, but it must have been associated with a change in the paint process at the factory.

During restoration, unpainted bulkheads are typically painted to match the rest of the bodyshell, not least as a way of protecting them in the longer term.

Front outer wings

The outer front wing panels on the Mk III Capri are visually similar to those on the Mk II models and are welded to the main bodyshell along the top and in the headlamp area. They are brazed on their lower edges to the front panel below the headlamp, and are retained under the valance by three M10 spire nuts.

As on a Mk II Capri, a good indicator of an original wing still in place is a 10mm nut and retaining plate that was used to locate the wing prior to welding on the assembly lines. The same reproduction panels will fit both Mk II and Mk III models, sometimes with a little intervention to correct the shape at the top rear, in front of the windscreen pillar. However, original Mk III wings also have a pressed metal bracket – known as the horseshoe – under the overhanging leading edge at the top.

A radio aerial was standard on GL models and above from the start of production in 1978, and was always fitted to the top of the left-hand front wing on right-hand-drive Capris for the UK market. On the early cars, it always had a matt black finish. However, an electrically-operated cast metal aerial with a chromed finish was standard on Ghia models and then on the 2.8 Injection from July 1981; this chromed electric aerial was also standard on Laser models from October 1984. These aerials were made specially for Ford by the Autu company.

CAPRI MK III DETAILS

All Mk III bonnets had the same "power bulge" regardless of engine size. This was a much-liked feature

Bonnet

The bonnet is sometimes described as being lower than that of the Mk II Capri, but this is an optical illusion brought about by its extra length. That extra length is all at the leading edge, where the bonnet forms an "eyebrow" over the headlamps and grille. All Mk III bonnets still had the "power bulge" that had been introduced to suit the extra height of the V6 engine, but which during the production of the Mk III became nothing more than a cosmetic feature.

All Mk III Capris had the same bonnet panel, and there were no changes to it during production. However, from April 1979 the S and Ghia models both gained better underbonnet sound insulation.

Scuttle panel

The Mk III scuttle panel is exactly the same as its equivalent on the Mk II Capri. A series of slots punched into it allow air to pass through and into the car's heating and ventilating system, and there are two holes for the wiper arm spindles. The wiper arms themselves are black on all Mk III Capris.

Doors

The doors are the same as on the Mk II Capris, with a steel outer skin clenched over a steel inner pressing. Into the cavity between the two is inserted the steel frame that forms the upper section of the door and carries the drop-glass. This is invariably painted black.

All the exterior door fittings are black, too. So the door handle and the finisher at the base of the window aperture are both black. The door handles themselves are otherwise the same as those used on the Capri Mk II, and on early cars incorporate the keylock. However, from 1983 the keylock is mounted separately, below the door handle itself; its escutcheon is of course black to match the rest of the door furniture. This change was made – somewhat belatedly –

Front bumpers on the Mk III models were quite different from earlier types, with inset turn indicator lamps and longer wraparounds. The shape of the lower apron panel with its integral spoiler is also clear here.

This close-up shows the scuttle panel with its slotted air intake vent, and the chrome-finished electric radio aerial that was used on models like this 280.

The keylock was mounted separately below the door handle on cars built from 1983. This example is on a 1985 Laser.

FACTORY-ORIGINAL FORD CAPRI MK II & MK III

This is the graduated side stripe on a 2.0 S model.

All early door mirrors had black bodies. This one is on a 1981 Calypso.

There were two types of mirror on the later cars. This one is the remote-control type, and has the pivot point some way down the stem. It is on a 1986 Laser.

This is the mirror without remote control, and its pivot is higher up, between the stem and the mirror body. It is on the passenger's side of a 1986 280 model.

because the earlier lock-and-handle unit could freeze up in cold weather.

All Capri Mk III models had at least a driver's door mirror, and all door mirrors on the early cars had black bodies. A passenger door mirror could be ordered as an extra-cost option for cars that did not have one as standard.

The L models came as standard with only a driver's door mirror. The GL also initially had only the one mirror, but came with a passenger's side mirror as well from the start of the 1980 model-year. The S models always had two mirrors. The Ghia initially had only the one mirror, but gained a second one for the 1980 model-year. The LS, Laser, Injection and Injection Special always had two mirrors.

A remotely controlled driver's door mirror was introduced in April 1979 for the 1980 model-year, adjusted by a toggle control in a round escutcheon just ahead of the interior door release handle. This was initially fitted only on the GL, S and Ghia models, became part of the LS specification when that model was introduced, and was always fitted to the 2.8-litre cars. The design of the remote-control mirror differs from that of the standard mirror, and the remote-control type is readily recognisable by a "break" in the stem. The standard type was never modified to match it, and as a result there is a mismatch when a passenger mirror is fitted with a remote-control driver's mirror. Remote adjustment was never available for the passenger's side door mirror.

On early cars, the extra weight of the adjustable mirror caused the door skin to split where it was crimped over the top of the inner panel, and on later cars a reinforcing panel was added behind the skin where the mirror is mounted.

Door mirrors with bodies painted to match the car's paintwork were introduced on the 2.8 Injection models from the beginning, and gradually spread further down the range. They became standard on the Laser models when these were introduced in October 1984.

Floorpan and Sills

There were no important differences between the Mk II floorpan and its Mk III equivalent. This was once again made of three sections, the front one including the transmission tunnel and having different panels at the front to suit manual or automatic gearboxes. The second section of the floopan then curves up and over the rear axle, and is welded to the third section, which includes the floor of the boot. There is side-to-side reinforcement from one cross-member below the front seat mounting position and from a second below the position for the rear seat.

A structural sill is welded to each side of the floorpan between the rear of the front wing and the front of the rear wheelarch. Each sill has an outer panel, an inner panel, and incorporates strengthening sections sandwiched between them. These sills are prone to corrosion and several aftermarket repair panels have been available over the years,

CAPRI MK III DETAILS

but not all are a very good fit.

On early Mk III cars, the lower safety belt mounting was on the inside panel of the sill, with the hole for the bolt directly below the door pillar. From autumn 1980, the position of the bolt hole in the sill was changed. This allowed a bar to be mounted inside the car which enabled the lower section of the belt to slide fore and aft.

Unlike those on the Mk II cars, the outer sills on the Mk III Capris are always finished in the body colour – or the lower body colour, in the case of cars with two-tone paintwork.

Windscreen pillars

On most Mk III Capris, the windscreen pillars were painted to match the rest of the bodywork. However, these pillars were painted black on the LS models (and also on the special-edition GT4; see p102).

Roof

There are rain gutters welded to the side of the roof above the windows, and these are painted to match the body. However, cars with a vinyl roof covering have a moulded black plastic trim that slides over the guttering.

A tilt-and-slide steel sunroof, always manually operated, was standard on Ghia models from the start of production, and on all cars with the 2.8-litre engine. It could also be ordered as an extra-cost option on L, GL and S models (but not on the entry-level 1300), and was used to add appeal to some of the special editions.

From March 1983, the sunroof became standard on the 1.6 LS and 2.0 S models. It remained standard on the 1.6 Laser and 2.0 Laser models. For details of its use on Special Edition models, please see the list of Special Editions at the end of this chapter.

From summer 1981, the sunroof could be ordered as part of an Executive Pack for all models except the Ghia. The other elements of this Executive Pack were an RST 21P radio-cassette head unit with speakers and an electric aerial.

On both the Mk I and Mk II Capris, a vinyl roof covering had been a popular option, and unsurprisingly one was also offered for the Mk III cars. However, it was very much less common on the Mk III models than on earlier types. It was always Black (although there were probably special orders, which should be provable if their ordering documentation has survived) and was an optional extra from the start on L, GL, S and Ghia models, but could not be had on the entry-level 1300. It was available with the LS specification but was withdrawn in August 1982 and was never offered for the 2.8-litre cars. It is always worth checking the provenance of a vinyl roof when possible, not least because enthusiasts have sometimes added one that was not original to a car.

The vinyl is glued in place on the steel roof panel. At the base of each rear pillar there is a horizontal finisher strip where the roof covering ends, with a matching strip below the rear window on the hatchback. A riveted extension plate extends the gutter line so that it lines up with the rear trim section, and there is then a moulded black plastic trim that slides over the guttering.

In cases where a vinyl roof was retro-fitted by a dealer – although there were relatively few examples of this – it was standard practice to use a clip in a plastic extension to avoid the need for drilling into the bodyshell.

Rear quarter-panels

The rear quarter-panels are integral to the main bodyshell, and are exactly the same as those on the Mk II cars. The right-hand quarter-panel contains the fuel filler flap on its sprung hinge. Behind this is of course the fuel filler cap itself, which from April 1982 was a locking type on all models from the 1.6L upwards.

When side decals and/or side bump rubbers are fitted, these continue across the rear quarter-panels, which are otherwise undecorated.

The fuel filler flap was in the right-hand rear quarter panel. Note the marking on the filler cap here: Ford never did think of these cars as Capri Mk IIIs but as facelifted Mk IIs!

The sunroof is pictured here in both open and closed conditions. Note the rubber seal on the leading edge of the sliding section, and the way it is visible all round the edge of the sunroof when the roof is closed.

FACTORY-ORIGINAL FORD CAPRI MK II & MK III

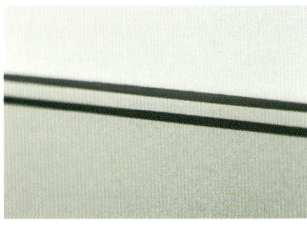

The Ghia models were the only ones to have this style of twin coachline, which was really a decal. The coachlines continue across the lower edge of the hatchback.

A quite different two-tone coachline was used for the Capri 280 models. Note how it terminates at the end of the wing panel and does not continue across the bottom of the tailgate.

The hatchback release was in a black escutcheon, but the rim of the keylock was not painted. Just visible here is one of the plastic plugs that concealed the attachment fixings for the spoiler.

The hatchback was a much-liked feature carried over from the Mk II models. The parcels shelf lifted with it – unless the supporting cables were detached – to give easier access to the boot area.

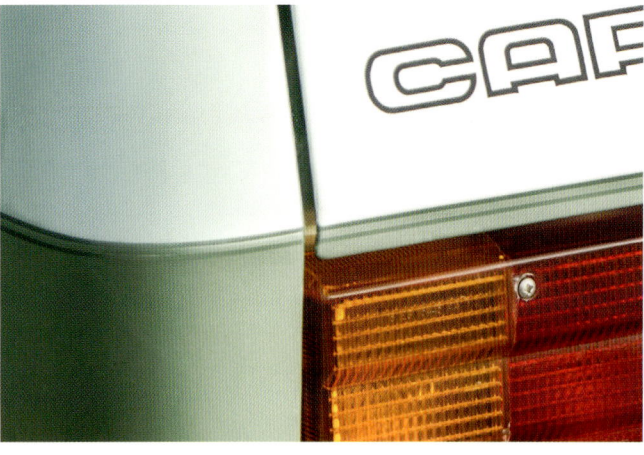

The underside of the hatchback shows how the trim panel was designed to fit around the wiper motor.

Hatchback

The hatchback is hinged from the roof panel and supported on either side by a gas strut, exactly as on the Mk II Capris. The combined keylock and press-button release is once again in the centre of the panel below the window, but on the Mk III everything is black except for the face of the keylock itself. The hinges were initially secured by 10mm bolts and nuts, but from January 1983 approximately, Torx splined fixings were used to reduce flexing of the hinge arms.

Several Mk III models have a black rubber spoiler on the trailing edge of the hatch. The fixings for this pass through the lower section of the spoiler and into the steel hatchback itself, and are concealed by black plugs. The spoiler is wider than the hatchback panel, and lies on top of the rear face of each quarter-panel when the hatchback is closed. Ford claimed that it reduced aerodynamic drag by 6.6%, in addition to the 6% gained from the chin spoiler. The spoiler was always fitted to S models, to the 1.6 LS from January 1981, to all models with the 2.8-litre engine and also all Laser models.

A wash-wipe system was available for the hatchback window. It was never available as part of the entry-level or L trim packages (although it could be ordered as an extra-cost option), but was standard on GL, S and Ghia models, and of course on all the LS and 2.8-litre cars as well. It was then made standard on both 1.6 and the 2.0 Laser models when these were introduced in October 1984.

This wash-wipe system was exactly the same as the Mk II type, with a black wiper arm mounted on a spindle just below the tailgate window and just left of centre. For details of the different types of wiper arms that were used, please see the later section on Windscreen Wipers.

Again as on the Mk II, the black plastic washer jet is located on the right-hand side of the roof, just above the hatchback.

A rear wiper was a feature of the better-equipped Mk III models. This is the later type, on a Capri Calypso, with the hook-type attachment for the wiper blade.

CAPRI MK III DETAILS

The rear bumper and spoiler are highlighted in these two pictures. The mudflaps on the 280 model are an aftermarket addition.

Tail panel and rear valance

The tail panel running below the hatchback opening is a simple pressing with a recessed centre where the number plate is mounted. It carries the rear light units and is always painted in the body colour.

The rear valance panel below the bumper curves at its outer edges to make a smooth join with the lower quarter-panels, unlike the Mk II design where there is a distinct step. From 1983, there is a cut-out in the centre of the panel on all models, which fits around a towing or lashing eye.

BODY FITTINGS

Bumpers

Both front and rear bumpers on Mk III Capris have a satin black paint finish, and have separate end-caps which wrap around the sides of the car to give additional protection. The front bumper has cut-outs to accommodate the turn signal lights, and the front number-plate is attached directly to the centre of the bumper, presenting a neater appearance than on the Mk II Capri.

The bumper end-caps were designed to reduce the cost of replacement after collision damage. They are separate plastic mouldings, and original items fit tightly and neatly to the bumpers. Some pattern replacement items do not fit as well, leaving a noticeable gap between end-cap and bumper.

Black over-riders were standard on S and Ghia models from the start, on all 2.8-litre variants, and on the Laser models introduced in October 1984. However, they could also be had as an extra-cost option for the L, GL and LS models.

A headlamp pressure-wash system was available as an extra-cost option on all Mk III Capris from the start of production. The units containing the washer jets were attached to the front bumper, and were the same as those used on contemporary Ford Cortina and Ford Granada models.

Radiator grille

The slatted radiator grille is unique to the Mk III Capri, and always carries a blue oval Ford badge in the centre. The grille panel is separate from the two mounting panels for the headlights. It is normally finished in black but from October 1984 the Laser and 2.8 Injection Special models have it painted in the body colour.

Glass and glazing

All Mk III models had a laminated windscreen from the start of production, and a heated rear window was a standard fitment across the range. All the glass is also rubber-glazed to the bodywork, except the opening rear quarter-lights (see below), which sit against a rubber seal when closed.

The glass in early Mk III Capris was a clear type except with the Ghia trim, when it always had a bronze tint. This tinted glass was optional on early L, GL and S models, but

The grille of the Mk III models carried a straightforward blue oval to identify its maker.

67

Opening rear quarter-vents were standard on some models and optional on others. Visible in this picture is the early style of door handle, without a separate keylock.

Period piece: aftermarket theft precautions were big business when the Mk III Capri was in production, and this window sticker on the 1981 Calypso model is an indication that the owner had tried to protect his car.

could not be had on the entry-level 1300. By summer 1981 it had become standard on the GL and the S models. It was also optionally available on the LS models, and subsequently became standard on all Capri models during 1983.

Rear quarter-windows

The rear quarter-windows were fixed in place on most models as Mk III production began, although opening windows were standard with the Ghia trim level.

These opening quarter-windows could be ordered as an option for the L, GL and LS models. They were standard on the GL as well by August 1981, standard on all 2.8-litre models from the start of their production in 1981, and became standard on the S models during 1983.

Body side trims

Like its Mk II predecessor, the Mk III Capri depended for its looks on creases in the body panels, which reduced the need for side adornments. Nevertheless, the body sides were not always plain.

At the bottom end of the model range, the base 1.3-litre model had a black belt moulding. In August 1981, three-piece side rubbing strips, moulded from black plastic, were introduced for all models except the 1300, LS and S variants. These were not quite aligned with the edges of the front and rear bumpers, and it is worth noting that the ones on the doors always looked a slightly different colour from the ones on the front wings and the rear quarters. (Pattern replacements have achieved a better colour match!) From January 1983, the rubbing strips were added to LS models, and from September 1984 they were standard on all the remaining models.

Body side decals

Decals were used quite widely on the Mk III Capri, both to distinguish mainstream models and to provide a simple and cost-effective way of adding an individual touch to some of the special editions.

The S models came as standard with a graduated stripe decal mounted on the body side level with the bumper wraparounds and accompanied by a letter S just ahead of each rear wheelarch. These decals were available in four different colours – Black, Silver, Light Argent or Dark Argent – to suit the main body colour.

For their last few months in production, the Ghia models had a twin coachline mounted just below the body side crease and running across the lower edge of the tailgate. These coachlines were added in March 1981 and were probably intended to help sell the final Ghia models before they gave way to the 2.8-litre cars after August 1981. It appears that there were 10 different colours of coachline, as follows:

Bright Blue	Light Blue
Brown	Light Green
Dark Argent	Light Grey
Dark Brown	Medium Green
Light Argent	Mid Red

Things became much more complicated with the LS models, which initially had a lower body side decal at bumper level. This decal was used only until August 1983, and thereafter was replaced by the three-piece plastic rubbing strip. There were 19 colour combinations, which were:

Medium Orange over Dark Red
Bright Blue over Mushroom
Light Red over Dark Red
Beige over Mushroom
Light Green over Dark Green
Airforce Blue over Light Argent
Light Orange over Dark Brown
Light Grey over Brick Red
Light Blue over Dark Blue
Light Green over Light Grey
Orange over Brown
Bright Blue over Mid Red
Blue over Dark Blue
Light Grey over Claret
Airforce Blue over Brick Red
Light Grey over Mid Red
Light Grey over Dark Blue
Metallic Grey over Claret
Bright Blue over Pink Red

Laser models had a double stripe decal just above the bump rubbers and level with the bumper wraparounds; the narrow upper stripe was solid but the broad lower one was graduated. The double stripe came in Light Argent or Dark

Argent, depending on the main body colour.

There were three different arrangements of side decals for the 2.8-litre cars, one for the early Injection models, one for the Injection Special models, and the third for the special edition 280. All of them had a twin coachline.

On the early 2.8 Injection models, the word "Injection" was all in lower-case letters and was set into the lower coachline, the tops of the letters being matched by "wiggles" in the upper coachline. There were three different coachline colours, of which one was short-lived:

Dark Argent over Mid Red
Light Argent over Mid Red
Mid Grey over Bright Red
(to August 1981 only, and therefore rare)

For the Injection Special models, the coachlines were altered so that they stopped short of the "Injection" decal with a downward turn. There were again three colour options:

Dark Red over Mid Argent
Dark Red over Mid Silver
Dark Red over White

The Capri 280 had a special arrangement, with twin narrow side stripes (one Dark Red, one White) broken by a Capri 280 identifier in the same two colours.

Front wing badges

The only hard badges mounted to the front wings of mainstream production Mk III Capris were the small shield type that distinguished the Ghia models. All other badges in this position were decals.

Laser models had a "Laser" decal on the front wing ahead of the decal stripes, and this was in Dark Argent with Claret or Light Argent with Claret. The various wing-mounted decals used on the 2.8-litre cars are described in the Body Side Decals section above, together with their coachlines.

This was the standard front wing identifier for the Capri Ghia.

Rear badges

All the mainstream Mk III Capri models had a blue Ford oval on the right-hand side of the hatchback's vertical lower edge. Unlike the other badges at the rear of the car, this was a hard plastic item that was glued in place.

All the other rear badges were decals, like those on the body sides and wings. The model identification badge was on the left of the hatchback at the bottom. It consisted of the Capri name in outlined capital letters, plus the engine size and the trim level. So, a typical example might have read "Capri 2.0 GL". On Ghia models, the Ghia identifier was in script rather than block letters, but once again the letters were outlined only and were not solid. On the Laser models, the trim level identifier was replaced by a "Laser" decal which had the same

This page from an early sales catalogue for the 2.8 Injection model illustrates both its "pepperpot" alloy wheels and the style of coachline and side decal that was used.

Some models also had identifiers on the front wings. This decal was used on the Capri Laser.

On the 280 Brooklands, the front wing identifier decal was located on the body crease.

The blue oval was also fitted to the right side of the tailgate on all models except the Tickford.

The 280 or Brooklands had a different layout of tailgate identifying decals.

colour combination as the Laser badges used on the car's front wings.

On cars with an automatic gearbox, there was an additional decal below the main one, reading "Automatic", and this came in Silver or Black to suit the body colour. However, on Ghia models (where an automatic gearbox was standard), the "Automatic" decal was deleted after summer 1980.

For the Capri 2.8 Injection models, the rear decal badge read "Capri 2.8 Injection" and was in one of three colour combinations, to match the side stripes. On the Capri 280 models, the left-hand side of the hatchback carried the same red and white decal as used on the front wings of these models.

The standard pattern for the tailgate decals on the left-hand side was model-engine size – trim level, as seen on all four of these examples.

PAINTS AND TRIMS, CAPRI MKIII

1979 model-year

At the introduction of the Mk III Capri, there were 15 colour options, consisting of eight solids, five metallics, and two Signal colours. Black, all Metallic colours and the two Signal paints were extra-cost options; Black was available only on the S. S models had tape side stripes in Black or Silver. When a vinyl roof covering was fitted, it was always Black, but the vinyl roof was not available on cars in Highland Green with Chocolate interior, or Fjord Blue with Tan interior.

All upholstery was cloth, and there were five different types, each allocated to a different trim level or model. The allocations and colour options were as follows:

1300	Beta Plus fabric
	Black, Chocolate, Red or Tan
L	Concord fabric with Savannah bolsters
	Black Savannah with Black and White Concord
	Chocolate Savannah with Black and Brown Concord
	Red Savannah with Black and White Concord
	Tan Savannah with Black and Brown Concord
GL	Diamond fabric
	Black, Chocolate, Red or Tan
S	Carla fabric with Savannah bolsters
	Black and White Carla with Black Savannah
	(Note: Launch sales material shows this with hints of red and blue in it; in practice, it had a very clear orange stripe)
	Brown and White Carla with Chocolate Savannah
	Red and White Carla with Black Savannah
Ghia	Verona fabric
	Black, Chocolate, Red or Tan

The full list of colour combinations is shown in the table below.

	L	1300, GL & Ghia	S	S tape stripe
Solids				
Alaskan Grey	Black or Red	Black or Red	Black or Red	Black
Black	(N/A)	(N/A)	Black or Red	Silver
Diamond White	Black or Chocolate	Black or Chocolate	Brown or Red	Black
Fjord Blue	Black or Tan	Black or Tan	Black	Silver
Highland Green	Black or Chocolate	Black or Chocolate	Black or Brown	Black
Midnight Blue	Black or Red	Black or Red	Black or Red	Silver
Nevada Beige	Chocolate or Tan	Chocolate or Tan	Black or Brown	Black
Venetian Red	Red or Tan	Red or Tan	Black or Red	Black
Metallics				
Hawaiian Blue	Black or Tan	Black or Tan	Black	Black
Jupiter Red	Black or Red	Red or Tan	Black or Red	Silver
Oyster Gold	Chocolate or Tan	Chocolate or Tan	Brown or Red	Black
Regency Green	Chocolate or Tan	Black or Tan	Black or Brown	Black
Strato Silver	Black or Red	Black or Red	Black or Red	Black
Signals				
Signal Amber	Chocolate or Tan	Black or Chocolate	Black or Brown	Black
Signal Yellow	Black or Chocolate	Black or Chocolate	Black or Brown	Black

1980 model-year (October 1979)

For the 1980 model-year that began in October 1979, there were 15 colour options, consisting of seven solids, five metallics, and two Signal colours plus Black. Black, all Metallic colours and the two Signal paints were extra-cost options. S models had tape side stripes in Black or Silver, and all vinyl roof coverings were Black.

All upholstery was cloth, and there were four different types, each allocated to a different trim level or model. There were three different base colours: Chocolate, Red and Tan. The model allocations of the different upholstery types were as follows:

L	Concord fabric with Savannah bolsters
GL	Windsor fabric
S	Carla fabric with Savannah bolsters
Ghia	Verona fabric

The full list of colour combinations is shown in the table below.

Solids	Interior option(s)
Cordoba Beige	Red or Tan
Corsican Blue	Tan
Diamond White	Chocolate or Red
Highland Green	Chocolate or Tan
Midnight Blue	Red or Tan
Tuscan Beige	Chocolate or Tan
Venetian Red	Red or Tan
Metallics	
Apollo Green	Chocolate or Tan
Cosmos Blue	Chocolate or Tan
Sirius Red	Chocolate or Tan
Solar Gold	Chocolate or Tan
Strato Silver	Chocolate or Red
Special orders	
Black	Tan, possibly also Red
Signal Red '80	Chocolate
Signal Yellow	Chocolate

(Signal Red was available only on the GT4 special edition.)

1981 (March)

The next round of changes occurred at the start of 1981, and the 2.8 Injection model was added while these options were still current, in July 1981. The 2.8 Injection had its own distinctive selection of colour and trim options.

There were initially 12 colour options, consisting of six solids and six metallics; three two-tone metallic options were added for the 2.8 Injection to bring the total up to 15. The metallic paints were standard on Ghia models in this period, but were extra-cost options on other models. The two-tone paint finishes cost extra on the 2.8 Injection. S models had tape side stripes in Black or Silver, and all vinyl roof coverings were Black.

All upholstery was cloth, and there were four different types, each allocated to a different trim level or model. There were five different base colours: Blue, Chocolate, Grey, Red and Tan. The model allocations of the different upholstery types were as follows:

L	Sandford fabric [large square pattern in weave]
GL	Windsor fabric
LS	Carla fabric with Savannah bolsters
S	Carla fabric with Savannah bolsters
Ghia	Verona fabric
2.8 Injection	Carla fabric with Savannah bolsters

The full list of colour combinations is shown in the tables below.

	L, GL, Ghia	S	LS
Solids			
Diamond White	Blue or Chocolate	Black or Red	Red
Dove Grey	Red or Tan	Black or Grey	Black
Meadow Green	Chocolate or Tan	Black or Grey	Grey
Midnight Blue	Blue or Tan	Black or Grey	Grey
Tuscan Beige	Chocolate or Tan	Black	Black
Venetian Red	Chocolate or Tan	Grey or Red	Red
Metallics			
Cobalt Blue	Blue or Tan	Black or Grey	Grey
Crystal Green	Chocolate or Tan	Black or Grey	Grey
Forest Green	Chocolate or Tan	Black or Grey	Grey
Graphite Grey	Blue or Tan	Black or Red	Red
Strato Silver	Blue or Chocolate	Black or Grey	Red
Tibetan Gold	Chocolate or Tan	Black	Black

2.8 Injection only (from July 1981)

There were eleven paint options, consisting of three solid colours, five metallics, and three two-tone combinations. Interiors were available in two colours only, Blue and Grey; the upholstery was Carla cloth with Dark Grey velour bolsters, and is commonly described as "Tartan".

Paint	Interior
Solids	
Diamond White	Blue or Grey
Midnight Blue	Blue
Venetian Red	Grey
Metallics	
Cobalt Blue	Blue
Crystal Green	Grey
Forest Green	Grey
Graphite Grey	Blue or Grey
Strato Silver	Blue or Grey
Two-tones	
Cobalt Blue over Strato Silver	Blue
Forest Green over Crystal Green	Grey
Graphite Grey over Strato Silver	Blue or Grey

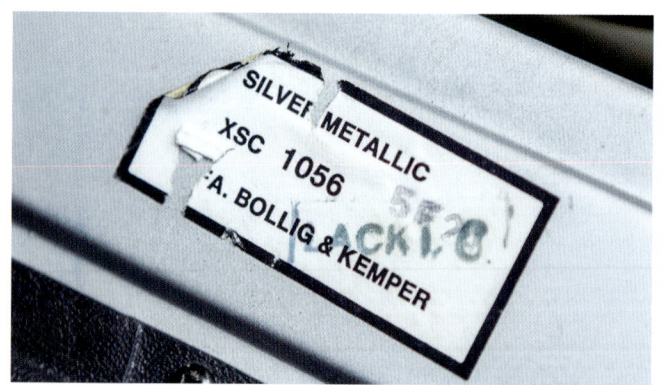

Paint stickers were made of paper and often do not survive. However, these examples, on a 1981 Calypso and a 1985 Laser, show what they looked like. The XSC number is a paint code, and "Fa Bollig & Kemper" indicates the supplier. "Fa" indicates "Firma" (company); Bollig & Kemper were and are major suppliers of paints and other automotive coatings, with headquarters in Cologne. Other paints were supplied by Sikkens.

1982, May

Further changes were made in May 1982. The 2.8 Injection again had its own distinctive selection of colour and trim options.

There were 17 colour options, consisting of seven solids and eight metallics, plus three two-tone metallic options for the 2.8 Injection. The metallic paints were standard on Ghia models in this period, but were extra-cost options on other models. The two-tone paint finishes cost extra on the 2.8 Injection and Black cost extra on all models. S models had tape side stripes in Black or Silver, and all vinyl roof coverings were Black.

All upholstery was cloth, and there were four different types, each allocated to a different trim level or model. The Sandford cloth used for the L models had a chequered pattern in the beginning but later changed to a plain finish. The Laser fabric on the S models had a grey or a red stripe.

The colour options and model allocations of the different upholstery types were as follows:

- L — Sandford fabric
  - Blue, Grey or Tan
- GL — York fabric
  - Blue, Grey or Tan
- LS — Carla fabric
  - Blue, Grey or Red
- S — Laser fabric
  - Blue, Grey or Red
- Ghia — Chelsea fabric
  - Blue, Grey or Tan
- 2.8 Injection — Carla fabric with velour bolsters
  - (this is often described as Tartan, to differentiate it from the earlier Carla fabric on the S models)
  - Grey

The full list of colour combinations is shown in the table below.

	L, GL and Ghia	LS and S	2.8 Injection
Solids			
Black	Blue or Grey	Grey	Grey
Cardinal Red	Grey or Tan	Grey	Grey
Caribbean Blue	Blue or Grey	Blue	(N/A)
Diamond White	Blue or Grey	Red	Grey
Dove Grey	Grey or Tan	Grey	(N/A)
Jasmine Yellow	Grey or Tan	Grey	(N/A)
Sienna Brown	Tan	Red	(N/A)
Metallics			
Celtic Bronze	Grey or Tan	Red	(N/A)
Champagne Gold	Grey or Tan	Grey	(N/A)
Crystal Green	Grey or Tan	Grey	Grey
Forest Green	Grey or Tan	Grey	Grey
Graphite Grey	Grey or Tan	Grey	Grey
Strato Silver	Blue or Grey	Grey	Grey
Titan Blue	Blue or Grey	Blue	Blue
Venus Gold	Tan	Grey	(N/A)
Two-tones			
Forest Green over Crystal Green	(N/A)	(N/A)	Grey
Graphite Grey over Strato Silver	(N/A)	(N/A)	Grey
Titan Blue over Strato Silver	(N/A)	(N/A)	Grey

1983, June

The considerably reduced Capri range available after May 1983 had a correspondingly reduced set of paint and trim options. The 2.8 Injection once again had its own distinctive selection.

There were 13 paint options, consisting of five solids and five metallics, plus three two-tone metallic options for the 2.8 Injection. Black, all metallic paints and the two-tones were all extra-cost options. All vinyl roof coverings were Black.

All upholstery was cloth, and there were three different types, each allocated to a different trim level or model.

The colour options and model allocations of the different upholstery types were as follows:

- LS — Carla fabric
  - Grey or Navy
- S — Laser fabric
  - Grey or Red
- 2.8 Injection — Monza fabric
  - with crushed velour bolsters
  - Grey

The full list of colour combinations is shown in the table below.

	1.6LS	2.0S (stripe)	2.8 Injection
Solids			
Black	Grey	Grey or Red	Grey
Cardinal Red	Grey	Grey or Red	Grey
Diamond White	Navy	Grey or Red	Grey
Ocean Blue	Navy	Grey or Red	(N/A)
Pine Green	Grey	Grey or Red	(N/A)
Metallics			
Caspian Blue	Navy	Grey or Red	Grey
Champagne Gold	Grey	Grey or Red	(N/A)
Glacier Blue	Navy	Grey	Grey
Nimbus Grey	Grey	Grey or Red	Grey
Strato Silver	Navy	Grey	Grey
Two-tones			
Caspian Blue over Strato Silver	(N/A)	(N/A)	Grey
Glacier Blue over Caspian Blue	(N/A)	(N/A)	Grey
Strato Silver over Nimbus Grey	(N/A)	(N/A)	Grey

1984, May

Some minor changes to the options were made in May 1984. The 2.8 Injection once again had its own distinctive selection.

There were 15 paint options, consisting of five solids and seven metallics, plus three two-tone metallic options for the 2.8 Injection. Black, all metallic paints and the two-tones were all extra-cost options. All vinyl roof coverings were Black.

All upholstery was cloth, and there were three different types, each allocated to a different trim level or model. The colour options and model allocations of the different upholstery types were as follows:

LS	Carla fabric Grey or Navy
S	Laser fabric Grey or Red
2.8 Injection	Monza fabric with crushed velour bolsters Grey

The full list of colour combinations is shown in the table below.

	1.6LS	2.0S (stripe)	2.8 Injection
Solids			
Black	Grey	Grey or Red	Grey
Cardinal Red	Grey	Grey or Red	Grey
Diamond White	Navy	Grey or Red	Grey
Ocean Blue	Navy	Grey	(N/A)
Pine Green	Grey	Grey or Red	(N/A)
Metallics			
Caspian Blue	Navy	Grey or Red	Grey
Champagne Gold	Grey	Grey or Red	(N/A)
Glacier Blue	Navy	Grey	grey
Havana Brown	Grey	Grey or Red	(N/A)
Jade Green	Grey	Grey or Red	(N/A)
Nimbus Grey	Grey	Grey or Red	Grey
Strato Silver	Navy	Grey or Red	Grey
Two-tones			
Caspian Blue over Strato Silver	(N/A)	(N/A)	Grey
Glacier Blue over Caspian Blue	(N/A)	(N/A)	Grey
Strato Silver over Nimbus Grey	(N/A)	(N/A)	Grey

1985 model-year (October 1984)

From October 1984, the 1985-model Capris were available with nine different paint options, consisting of three solids and four metallics, plus two two-tone metallic options that were available on all models. All paint options were available on both the Laser and the 2.8 Injection Special. Black, all metallic paints and the two-tones were all extra-cost options. All vinyl roof coverings were Black.

There were two different types of upholstery, each allocated to a different model. There was no choice of colour in either case:

Laser	Truro II fabric (Grey) with Grey fabric bolsters
2.8 Injection	Strobe fabric (Black and Grey) with Shark Grey leather bolsters

The full list of colour combinations is shown in the table below.

Solids
Black
Diamond White
Lacquer Red

Metallics
Mineral Blue
Nimbus Grey
Paris Blue
Strato Silver

Two-tones
Mineral Blue over Strato Silver
Nimbus Grey over Strato Silver

1986, April

There was a minor change in April 1986, when Rosso Red was added to make the number of solid paint options up to four and the total paint options up to ten. All the other paints were the same as they had been before.

1986, November

The final set of paint options affected only the very last Capris to be built. It was introduced in November 1986 and production ended at Cologne in December.

There were three new colours and two new two-tone combinations, and the total of paint options was nine. Black, the metallic colours and the two-tones were all extra-cost options. Laser models again had Truro II fabric upholstery, always in Grey with Grey fabric bolsters, and the 2.8 Injection Special again had Strobe fabric seats in Black and Grey, with Shark Grey leather bolsters.

The three solid colours and four metallics were available on both Laser and 2.8 Injection Special models. The two two-tone combinations were available on the 2.8 Injection Special but were not normally available on the Laser (although a small number do appear to have been supplied to special order).

The paint colours were as follows:

Solids
Black
Diamond White
Rosso Red

Metallics
Crystal Blue
Mercury Grey
Regency Red
Strato Silver

Two-tones
Crystal Blue over Strato Silver
Mercury Grey over Strato Silver

CAPRI MK III DETAILS

The headlight casing was moulded from black plastic and was left unpainted on early cars, to match the back grille.

LIGHTING

Headlights and sidelights

One of the most obvious differences between the Mk III models and the Mk IIs that they replaced lay in the headlights, which on the Mk III were always four round halogen units with a 5¾in diameter. These were set into a plastic surround panel which matched the depth of the grille; the headlamp surrounds were normally black, but were painted in the body colour on some later models which also had body-colour grilles. There were no separate sidelight units; instead, there was an 8-watt "pilot" sidelight in each outer headlamp.

The headlights are mounted in a metal baseplate and can be adjusted by screws within the baseplate. Each one is held to the baseplate by a retaining ring. The outer headlamp is for dipped beam and the inner one for main beam. From October 1986, the headlamps on UK-market cars were controlled by a "dim-dip" system to meet new legislation; this meant that the main and dipped beams were automatically extinguished when the ignition was turned off. Cars with the "dim-dip"

Later cars had the grille and headlamp casings in the body colour. However, these items were not mounted to the bodyshell before it passed through the paint shop: note how the fixing screws remained unpainted.

When headlamp washers were fitted, as on this 3.0-litre Ghia, the jet unit was mounted on top of the front bumper.

FACTORY-ORIGINAL FORD CAPRI MK II & MK III

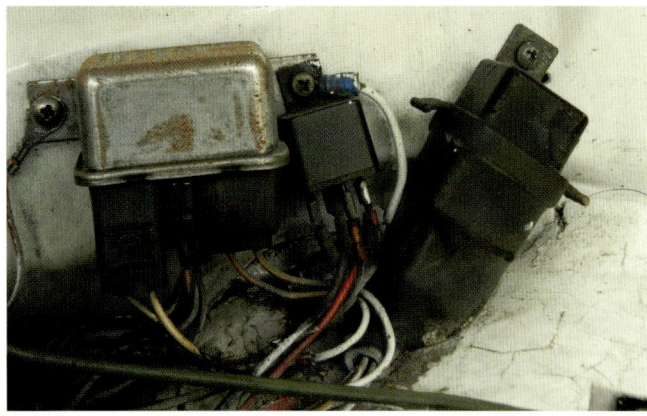

Later cars with the dim-dip headlight system had this additional relay (right) on the bulkhead.

system have an additional relay on the bulkhead, and also have relays mounted underneath the radiator air duct panel.

Headlamp washers were an option on S and Ghia models from the start of production. They became standard for the Ghia in April 1979 for the 1980 model-year, but remained an extra-cost option (and therefore rare) on all other models. The add-on washer unit consisted of a black plastic moulding that was attached to the bumper in front of each pair of headlights. Each one contained adjustable twin washer jets and was fed by a washer tube from underneath and behind the bumper.

Front and side direction indicators

The front direction indicators are mounted in the bumper and the same unit is used on each side. They are secured by screws through the projecting top of the light unit and each has a 21-watt bulb.

Side indicator repeater lights became standard on all Capris destined for the UK from February 1986. These have a small "square" amber lens and each one carries a 4-watt bulb.

Auxiliary lighting

As was the case with the Mk II cars, auxiliary lighting was generally uncommon on these later Capris. In theory, fog lamps and long-range driving lamps could be ordered as accessories, in each case manufactured by Hella. They were mounted on brackets that bolted to pre-drilled holes in the front valance, below the bumper, but never looked particularly attractive – which may help to explain why they remained uncommon.

Rear lights

The Mk III tail lights were larger than those on earlier Capris, and they were handed, with plastic lenses that were ribbed in the style of those that were then being introduced on all European Fords. The principle of the ribbed design appears to have originated with Mercedes-Benz, who introduced them on the W116 S Class saloons in 1972, and the theory was that the ribs prevented the whole lens being obscured by road dirt; the inset areas would remain clean. The Ford version actually had a rather different design that was more like the timbers of a clinker-built boat hull, but seemed to work nearly as well – and looked stylish into the bargain.

These lights had plastic lenses attached by screws to a backing plate that contained the bulbs. There was a gasket between backing plate and lens unit. There were also two different versions of the tail lamp assembly, one with a fog guard lamp and the other without. In the beginning, the fog guard lamps were standard only on GL and Ghia models; from April 1979 they became standard on the S models, and then filtered down to the L variants as well for the 1980 model-year. They were never available on the entry-level 1300. During the 1980s, they were standard on all the new Capri variants.

All light assemblies were divided into five distinct sections; on cars without rear fog guard lights, the relevant section simply had neither bulb nor wiring. The five sections were for the fog guard light, reversing light, reflector, combined tail light and brake light, and the direction indicator. The reversing lights were operated automatically by a plunger switch on the gearbox; the switch changed to a different type with the same function in March 1982.

There were also two number-plate illumination bulbs mounted above the plate itself in housings that were screwed to the lip of the hatch opening.

The rear light units were larger than those on the Mk II cars and featured ribbed lenses. As will be apparent from these pictures, the lenses were also handed.

CAPRI MK III DETAILS

ELECTRICAL

The electrical system is a 12-volt type with a negative earth on all models of Mk III Capri.

Battery and charging system

The battery is mounted under the bonnet. On all four-cylinder models and the 3.0-litre V6 cars, it is adjacent to the left-hand inner wing (or on the right of someone standing in front of the car and looking at the engine). However, on the 2.8-litre models the battery is relocated against the inner wing on the opposite side. (On the Tickford models it is relocated altogether, and is in the boot.)

Different battery capacities were needed for different models. The 1.3-litre, 1.6-litre and 2.0-litre manual models all have 35Ah batteries. Automatic versions of these cars, plus the manual-gearbox 3.0-litre, have a bigger 44Ah battery. Ford specified a 55Ah battery for all 3.0-litre models with an automatic gearbox, and for all the 2.8-litre cars. The standard alternator on most models had a 45 amp output, but the 2.8-litre cars had a much more powerful alternator with a 70 amp output to deal with greater electrical loads. It is certainly advisable – and Ford dealers would probably have advised it when the cars were new – to uprate the alternator and the battery on any car fitted with electrical accessories like auxiliary driving lamps or a modern in-car entertainment system

The fuse box is mounted on a shelf that projects forwards from the bulkhead, and is on the right of the car (the left when looking into the engine bay). It has a black plastic cover and contains seven fuses.

Windscreen wipers and washers

All Mk III Capris came with a two-speed windscreen wiper system that also incorporated an intermittent setting. The pivots for the wiper arms emerge from the scuttle panel in the usual Capri fashion, and the arms themselves fit over them

The original type of battery posts looked like this. Both of these were pictured on a 1985 Laser model.

and are secured by a nut.

The wiper arms are invariably black, and should park neatly at the base of the windscreen on the passenger's side. There were two changes of type during Mk III production. The first change occurred in the first quarter of 1980, when the original hook-type fixing for the wiper arm changed to a spigot-type fixing. The two types of arm are interchangeable, but their associated blade carriers are obviously not. No precise changeover date can be established, although most cars built from April 1980 had the later type; it appears that the change occurred gradually as supplies of the earlier arms ran out on the production lines. Some cars had both: at least one GT4 special-edition model (introduced in March 1980) had the old hook-type arms for the windscreen and a spigot type for the hatchback.

The second change occurred during 1982, and in this case affected the plastic flip cover over the securing nut. Early ones had a rounded end and were a tight fit over the nut, which caused them to split; so the cover was changed on the later ones to a squarer type that gave more clearance around the nut.

The standard washer bottle is a plastic type and, on most four-cylinder and 3.0-litre V6 models, is located on a bracket mounted to the right-hand inner wing (on the left when looking into the engine bay). On the 2.8-litre cars, the bottle is located on the left-hand front face of the bulkhead (right-hand when looking at the engine), because the repositioned battery occupies the standard mounting position. On four-cylinder and 3.0-litre cars fitted with headlamp washers, a larger reservoir is fitted in the standard position; this one has a distinctive notch in its rear face.

Horns

From the start of production, Ghia models had two-tone horns, but all other models had a single-tone horn.

Wiper arms were invariably black, as seen on this Calypso model. These are the early arms, with hook-type fixing and tight-fitting caps over the pivots

77

FACTORY-ORIGINAL FORD CAPRI MK II & MK III

The 1.6-litre Pinto engine is seen here in a 1981 Calypso. The original cast manifolds tend to crack, and this engine has been fitted with an aftermarket tubular type – a sensible modification in the circumstances. The ignition leads are also replacements, and would probably have been black when the car was new.

ENGINE IDENTIFICATION

Engine numbers consist of a two-letter prefix plus a five-digit serial number that matches the car's chassis number. The two-letter prefix is a date code, and can be interpreted by using the date codes shown in Appendix A. So (for example) an EB prefix would indicate an engine built in January 1984.

The engine number is die-stamped into a raised casting on the cylinder block on the right-hand side of all engines (left-hand side when standing looking into the engine bay).

ENGINE, FUEL SYSTEM AND EXHAUST

When the Mk III cars were introduced in March 1978, Ford claimed that careful carburettor calibration had contributed to fuel savings of up to 10% (some of this 10% would have been attributable to the aerodynamic improvements, of course). However, the fact is that all the engines in the first cars except for the 1.3-litre were unchanged from their Mk II form. So perhaps that information about recalibrated carburettors should be taken with a pinch of salt!

1.3-litre

The engine in the Capri 1300 was the 1298cc Kent overhead-valve four-cylinder, as originally used in the Mk I Capri and now rather long in the tooth. The carburettor was a Motorcraft GPD (single venturi downdraught) type, the compression ratio was 9.2:1, and power on the first engines was 57bhp at 5500rpm while torque was quoted as 67 lb ft at 3000rpm. Interestingly, the final Mk II versions of this engine had what was described as an economy tune and delivered only 50bhp with 64 lb ft of torque; engines built before February 1976 had the same 57bhp and 67 lb ft as the "new" Mk III types!

From autumn 1979 in the showrooms for the 1980 model-year (but from April on the production lines), these engines had several minor revisions that autumn that were intended to reduce fuel consumption. They were given low-friction piston rings, revised valve spring settings, a viscous-coupled cooling fan and a variable-venturi Motorcraft carburettor. These later engines had 60bhp at 5750rpm with torque of 68 lb ft at 3000rpm.

These engines were withdrawn in autumn 1981 when the 1.3-litre models went out of production for the UK.

1.6-litre standard

The 1.6-litre engine was the 1593cc Pinto overhead-camshaft four-cylinder, carried over from the Mk II Capri and used earlier in the last Mk I models. It came in both standard and high-performance (1.6 S) versions.

The standard versions in early Mk III Capris had a Motorcraft GPD (single venturi downdraught) carburettor and a 9.2:1 compression ratio. The 1979-model engines delivered

CAPRI MK III DETAILS

This is the 2.0-litre Pinto engine in a 1985 Laser model. Note the much larger air cleaner on this engine, with its intake trumpet in this case pointing straight ahead towards the radiator. Clear in this picture is the unpainted bulkhead of many later Mk IIIs.

This is the exhaust side of the 2.0-litre Pinto engine, this time in a 1986 Laser model and with the exhaust inlet trumpet turned down to draw in warm air from above the exhaust manifold. The black cylindrical item just inside the wing is a 1980s anti-theft alarm system.

72bhp at 5500rpm with 87 lb ft of torque at 2700rpm. An automatic choke was added in April 1979.

There were then revisions in autumn 1979 for the 1980 model-year, as these engines gained similar improvements to those on the 1.3-litre types: low-friction piston rings, revised valve spring settings, a variable-venturi carburettor and a viscous-coupled cooling fan. With these changes came only marginally revised power and torque figures of 73bhp at 5300rpm and 86 lb ft at 2700rpm, but with a claimed improvement in fuel economy.

The final Capri versions of these engines were used in the 1.6-litre Laser models from October 1984.

1.6-litre S

Ford often described the high-performance version of the 1.6 Pinto engine as the GT type, even though the only version of the Capri that it powered was not called a GT but rather a Capri S.

Most of the differences between the GT engine and the standard 1.6-litre Pinto were at the top end. The GT versions

79

FACTORY-ORIGINAL FORD CAPRI MK II & MK III

Genuine Ford consumables, such as this fan belt on a 2.0-litre engine, carried Motorcraft branding.

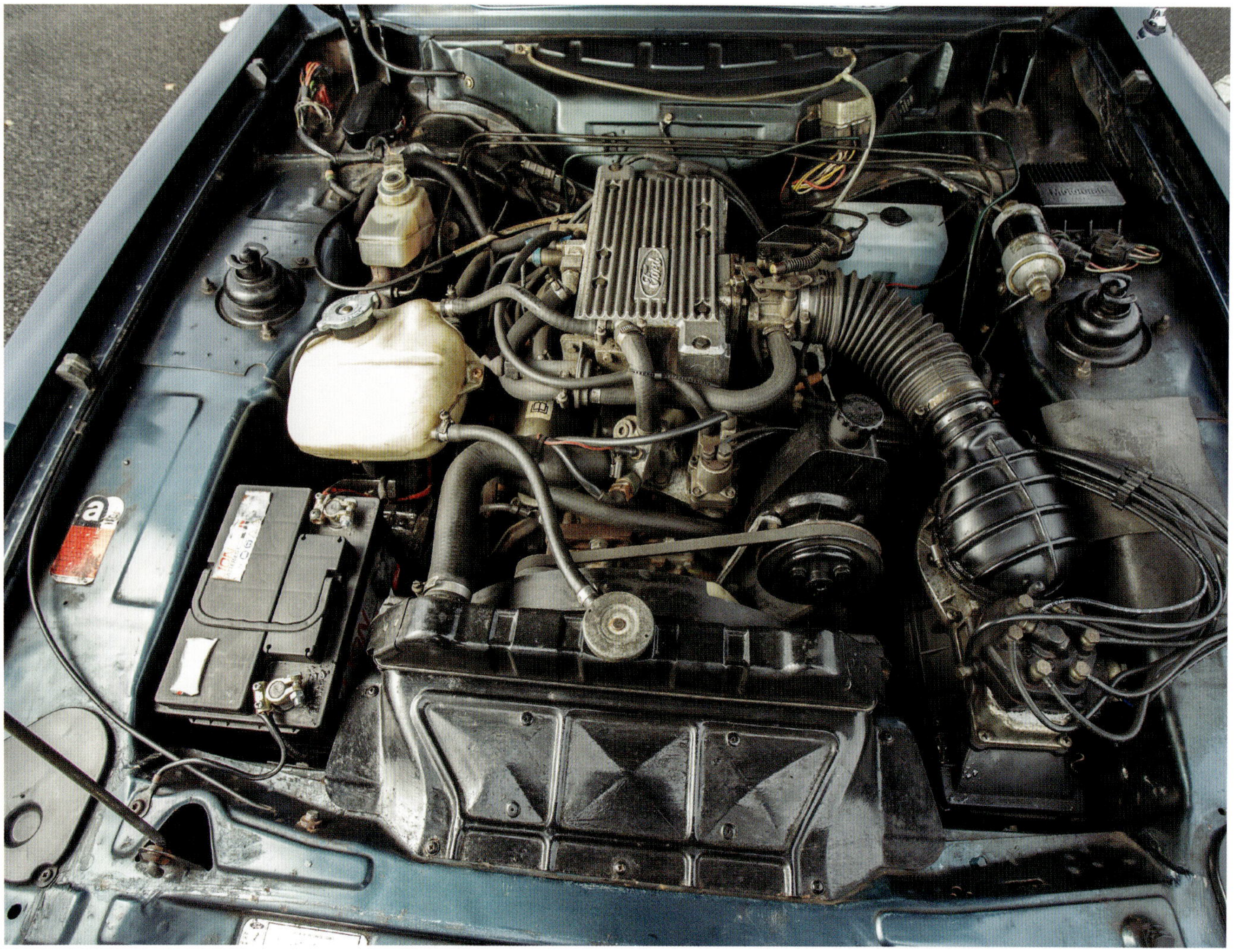

The 2.8-litre V6 with its petrol injection system presents a very different underbonnet picture. The battery has also changed sides to make way for the rotary injection pump, and the ducting panel behind the radiator is different from earlier types. The injection pipes tended to chafe on the inner wing, and the owner has fitted a large rubber pad to prevent this; only the smaller pad was fitted when the cars were new.

had a twin-choke (twin sequential chokes) Weber 32/36DGV carburettor with automatic choke and a 9.2:1 compression ratio. On the 1979-model engines, they put out 88bhp at 5700rpm and 92 lb ft at 4000rpm, and gained a viscous-coupled fan in April 1979. Low-friction piston rings and revised valve spring settings that autumn for the 1980 model-year improved power to 91bhp at 5900rpm, while the quoted torque figure remained unchanged.

2.0-litre

The 1994cc engine in the 2000 models was again a Pinto overhead-camshaft four-cylinder and was again carried over from the Mk II Capris. The carburettor was a twin-choke Weber 32/36DGV type with an automatic choke, although this has larger-diameter primary jets than the similar carburettor on the 1.6-litre S engine (and will cause over-fuelling if fitted to the smaller-capacity engine). The figures for 1979-model engines were 98bhp at 5200rpm and 112 lb ft at 3500rpm.

A viscous-coupled fan was fitted from April 1979, and then the autumn 1979 revisions – low-friction piston rings, revised

The 3.0-litre V6 engine had a metal-bodied air filter with its intake trumpet permanently positioned over the left-hand exhaust manifold. Clear in these pictures is the larger washer bottle next to the inner wing, which was needed to supply the headlamp washers as well as those for the windscreen.

valve spring settings, and a viscous-coupled cooling fan – improved power to 101bhp at the same engine speed, while maximum torque remained unchanged. In this final state of tune, the 2.0-litre engine was also used in the Capri Laser models from summer 1984.

2.8-litre

The 2.8-litre or "Cologne" V6 engine was made available in July 1981 and replaced the 3.0-litre Essex V6 as the largest engine in the Capri range. It was shared with the contemporary Ford Granada. This was a 2792cc 60-degree V6, with a 93mm bore and a 68.5mm stroke. The compression ratio was 9.2:1 and fuelling was achieved through a Bosch K-Jetronic injection system. The power and torque figures, which remained the same until the end of Capri production, were 160bhp at 5700rpm and 162 lb ft at 4300rpm.

3.0-litre

The Essex 3.0-litre V6 was another carry-over engine that had first been used in the Mk I Capris. Still with 2994cc, it had a

twin-choke (synchronous chokes) Weber 38/38EGAS carburettor with automatic choke and a 9.0:1 compression ratio, and delivered 138bhp at 5000rpm with 174 b ft of torque at 3000rpm. From April 1979, this engine had the viscous-coupled fan that was standardised on all Capri engines then in production.

Ford had said at the launch of the Mk III Capri that the 3.0-litre V6 engine would remain in production until 1981, and that prediction turned out to be very accurate. The final examples of the old Essex engine appear to have been built at the end of 1980, and powered cars that passed through the showrooms in the first half of 1981. Their replacement was the more powerful and more refined 2.8-litre Cologne V6, described above.

Fuel system

Two types of fuel tank are fitted to Capri Mk III models, one for the carburettor engines and the other for the injected 2.8-litre engine. Both have the same "13-gallon" capacity, which in practice is 58 litres or 12.7 gallons. Each tank is secured to the bodyshell behind the rear seat by a pair of metal straps.

The carburettor-type tank is the same as the one on later Capri Mk II models with a side exit and side-mounted fuel sender unit. Fuel delivery to the engine depends on a mechanical diaphragm-type pump. The injection-type tank is visually similar but has an internal swirl pot and a take-off spout for the high-pressure electric fuel pump.

Exhaust

It is highly unlikely that many Mk III Capri models still have an original-specification exhaust system. One reason is that the original types are now hard to find, and another is that aftermarket exhaust makers have tended to focus on modified systems that release extra power – or, at the very least, sound more powerful.

Original-specification exhaust systems for the four-cylinder cars were all single-pipe types that terminated in a single outlet pipe on the left side of the car. All of them have three main sections: a front pipe connected to the manifold, a centre silencer box and associated pipework, and a rear section with pipework, silencer and tailpipe. However, the individual components of the system differ from model to model.

Both V6 models have a full-length twin-pipe system with an exhaust tailpipe on either side of the car. The two systems again share a similar layout, with front pipes from the manifolds, centre sections incorporating a main silencer, and rear pipes with a smaller back box that leads to a tailpipe on either side of the car below the rear valance. However, the systems for the 2.8-litre and 3.0-litre engines are not interchangeable.

Transmission

There were three basic types of gearbox available on the Mk III Capri models. The manual option was initially a four-speed type, but a five-speed became available on 2.8-litre models during 1983 and then filtered down to 2.0-litre and 1.6-litre types later the same year. It was never available with the 1.3-litre engine. The automatic gearbox was a three-speed type and was available with all engines from the 1.6-litre upwards, but never with the 1.3-litre size.

Manual gearbox

The four-speed gearbox used on the 1.3-litre and 1.6-litre models was a Ford Type C. The four-speed gearbox for the 2.0-litre models was a Ford Type H (with three external rod linkages), and the one that accompanied both V6 engines was a Ford Type E.

The five-speed manual gearbox was a Ford Type 9, and was based on the company's four-speed Type E gearbox, with the

Four-cylinder models had a single exhaust tailpipe, which emerged on the left-hand side of the car.

The V6 models had twin tailpipes, which emerged one on either side of the car. This is how the layout looked on a 3.0-litre Ghia model.

The twin tailpipes are seen here on a later 2.8-litre V6 car.

overdrive fifth gear located in an extension housing at the rear. This gearbox replaced the four-speed Type E on 2.8-litre models in January 1983; in March that year it replaced the four-speed with the 2.0-litre engine; it was optional for the 1.6 LS; and then from October 1984 it was also available with the 1.6-litre engine in the Capri Laser models.

The gear ratios were as follows:

	1.3 & 1.6 4-speed Type C	2.0 4-speed Type H	1.6 & 2.0 5-speed Type 9	2.8 & 3.0 4-speed Type E	2.8 5-speed Type 9
1	3.58:1	3.65:1	3.65:1	3.16:1	3.36:1
2	2.01:1	1.97:1	1.97:1	1.94:1	1.81:1
3	1.397:1	1.37:1	1.37:1	1.412:1	1.26:1
4	1.00:1	1.00:1	1.00:1	1.00:1	1.00:1
5	–	–	0.816:1	–	0.825:1
Rev	3.324:1	3.16:1	3.660:1	3.346:1	3.365:1

Clutch

Like the Mk II models, the Mk III Capris had several different varieties of clutch, although all were diaphragm-spring, single dry plate types.

With the 1.3-litre and standard 1.6-litre engines, the clutch was made by LUK and had a 7.5in (190mm) diameter. For the 1.6 S models, clutches were made by either LUK or by Fichtel & Sachs, and had a larger 8.5in (216mm) diameter; this size of clutch was also used for the 2.0-litre models. The 3.0-litre and later 2.8-litre V6 models all had 9.5in (242mm) clutches, by Fichtel & Sachs. Clutch linings were made by Textar (with their 50S/17 specification) or Ferodo (their 2124F type), and the 9.5in clutches on the two V6 cars could also have a Mintex H26 lining.

Automatic gearbox

The three-speed Ford C3 gearbox was the automatic option, as it had been for the Mk II Capri, and always came with its own oil cooler. It was available only with the 1.6-litre, 2.0-litre and 3.0-litre engines; there was no automatic option for the 1.3, 1.6 S, or any of the 2.8-litre models. The two 3-litre models (3.0 S and 3.0 Ghia), had the automatic gearbox as standard, although from the start of Mk III production in 1978 it was possible to order the 3.0 Ghia with a manual gearbox (and Ford actually reduced the price slightly on such special orders).

The gear ratios for all versions of the C3 automatic were the same, at 2.474:1, 1.474:1 and 1.000:1. The Reverse ratio was 2.111:1.

Rear axle and final drive

All rear axles had a banjo casing that enclosed a semi-floating hypoid final drive. However, there were two major types of axle. The 1.3 and standard 1.6 models had the Timken Type J axle, while the 1.6 S and all 2.0-litre, 2.8-litre and 3.0-litre models had the stronger Salisbury Type D axle.

There was no limited-slip differential option available at the start of Mk III Capri production, but an LSD was made standard on the 2.8 Injection Special and the Capri 280 models.

The final drive ratios were as follows:
1.3-litre models	4.125:1
1.6-litre models	3.770:1
1.6 S models	3.750:1
2.0-litre models	3.440:1
2.8-litre models	3.090:1
3.0-litre models	3.090:1

The same ratios were used with four-speed manual, five-speed manual, and three-speed automatic gearboxes.

SUSPENSION

The layout of the front suspension was the same as it had been on the Mk II Capris, with MacPherson struts, lower track-control arms and an anti-roll bar. On all early four-cylinder models, the anti-roll bar has a 22mm diameter, but on all V6 models and on the LS and all Laser models there is a 24mm anti-roll bar.

The rear axle was again suspended on semi-elliptic springs and located by its own anti-roll bar. The rear anti-roll bar has a 12mm diameter on all early four-cylinder Mk III models, but the 3.0-litre models always had a thicker 14mm bar. This 14mm anti-roll bar was standard on the 2.8-litre models from the start of their production. In 1983 it was also fitted to the 2.0 S, and subsequently became standard on all Laser models as well.

All models had gas-filled telescopic rear dampers except for the entry-level 1.3-litre types, which had oil-filled strut inserts and rear dampers; the Laser models had Sachs gas dampers at the rear but oil-filled strut inserts at the front. The 3.0 models had stiffer springs (which Ford rather grandly described as "uprated suspension"), and from 1981 these were also fitted to the 1.6 LS and 2.0 S models.

The 2.8 Injection models came with a suspension drawn up by Ford's Special Vehicle Engineering division, which is sometimes known as the SVE suspension. Their ride height was lowered by 37mm to improve handling, and there were stiffer road springs, Bilstein gas dampers and strut inserts, and the thicker anti-roll bars described above (14mm at the front and 24mm at the rear). A slightly modified version of this suspension became standard on the 2.0 S models from March 1983.

Steering and brakes

Rack-and-pinion steering was again used, with power assistance as standard on the 3.0 S and 3.0 Ghia models. It could be deleted from either of those to special order – and Ford would reduce the showroom price accordingly. Power steering was also standard on the 2.8-litre cars, but for these there was no delete option.

Disc brakes were standard on the front wheels of the Capri Mk III. Clear here is the strut of the MacPherson front suspension.

The eight-spoke alloy wheel used on Ghia models had a quite ornate but very attractive design. Wheel nuts were chromed, as here, and the wheel centre caps were silver.

This is a four-spoke alloy wheel on a 1981 Capri Calypso. The wheel nuts are domed, except for the single aftermarket locking nut. The wheel centre cap is silver.

The same style of wheel on this 1985 Laser has a different style of aftermarket locking nut and, this time, a black centre cap.

Like earlier Capris, the Mk IIIs had disc brakes on the front wheels and drum brakes at the rear. Inspection panels in brake back plates make it easy to check how worn the linings are on rear drums. All models had a vacuum servo and dual-line hydraulic brake systems.

The rear brake drums on 1.3-litre and 1.6-litre "standard" models had an 8.5-inch diameter, but the 1.6 S and 2.0-litre cars had larger-diameter 9-inch drums. There were also 9-inch drums on the 3.0-litre cars, but these were wider than the type used on the smaller-engined cars. The 2.8-litre models had ventilated front brake discs, plus "improved" pad and lining material all round, and a G-valve load limiter in the hydraulic line to the rear wheels.

WHEELS AND TYRES

Most wheels on the Mk III Capri range had a 13-inch diameter, but a 15-inch size was available only on the final Capri 280 models. All types had a four-bolt fixing. The notes that follow show the standard factory specifications, but in most cases it was possible to order wheels from a higher-specification model at extra cost. An exception to this rule was that the 13-inch and 15-inch RS wheels were not available as options outside the cars on which they were standard.

Standard wear for the L models were styled steel types with oval holes and 5J (5-inch) rims; these wheels were always painted silver and had large black rubber conical centre caps. There was a second version of these with the same style but

This style of 15-inch wheel was unique to the Capri 280. The wheel nuts are concealed behind the lockable central disc, which carries a Ford oval logo.

Among the markings cast into the spokes of the four-spoke alloy wheels is a date of manufacture. This is the spare wheel of a 1985-model Laser.

with 5.5J (5.5-inch) rims, and these were used on GL models from October 1980. They had the same black centre cones but on the GL came with detachable bright trim rings. For the LS models, there was a new design of steel wheel. This was again painted silver and had a 5.5-inch rim, but there were eight round holes as perforations and the centre cap was a broad type in silver that was styled to fit around the securing nuts.

The more expensive Capri models came with alloy wheels as standard, and there were four different designs, of which one was available in two different sizes. The narrowest of these wheels had a 5.5J (5.5-inch) rim and a most attractive design with eight deeply dished spokes. This was the standard wheel for all Ghia models, and was also standard on the S models between 1978 and 1980. These wheels always had bright metal centre caps.

Next up in size came a four-spoke alloy wheel with a 6J (6-inch) rim. This was introduced in summer 1980 (the parts catalogue shows a June 1980 start to production) for the S models, and from October 1984 was standard on the Laser models.

For the first 2.8-litre models, Ford standardised a new design of alloy wheel with a 7J (7-inch) rim size. This had a "pepperpot" design with 12 holes in its face, and is correctly known as the Wolfrace Sonic type. The eight holes in the outer ring went right through the wheel disc, but the inner four concealed the wheel fixing nuts.

There were then two more alloy wheels, each with 7J (7-inch) rims and a seven-spoke design. The earlier type had a 13-inch diameter and was standard on the 2.8 Injection Special models; the later had a 15-inch diameter and, as noted above, was unique to the Capri 280 models. These wheels originated with Ford's RS performance division, but on the Capri they did not carry RS logos because the Injection Special was not an RS product. Both sizes of this wheel had a large central disc bearing the Ford logo and covering the wheel nuts, and that disc could only be removed with the aid of a special key. These wheels are therefore often described as "lockable" types.

Ford did not supply locking nuts for any of the wheel designs used on the Mk III Capri. Nevertheless, many owners at the time fitted aftermarket types to deter thieves, and enthusiast owners today often do the same.

The situation with tyres was no less complicated than that with the wheels. The 1.3 L and 1.6 L models with 5J steel wheels came with 165SR13 tyres. There were also 165SR13 tyres for the 5.5J steel wheels on 1.3 GL and 1.6 GL models, but when these wheels were fitted to the 2.0 GL they came with 185/70SR 13 tyres. There were also 185/70SR13 tyres for the 1.6 LS models.

All the S and Ghia models had 185/70HR13 tyres with their higher speed rating, but if the 6J alloys associated with these models were ordered for an L or GL model, they came with 185/70SR13 tyres instead. Finally, the 13-inch RS wheels came with 205/60x13 Goodyear NCT tyres as original equipment, and the 15-inch RS wheels came with 195/50x15 Pirelli P7 tyres.

FACTORY-ORIGINAL Ford Capri MK II & MK III

The two-dial dashboard was used on lower-specification models, and this Ford publicity picture also shows the herringbone cloth used for the seats. Note the rather gratuitous fluting on the passenger's side of the dash, the overall grey finish for the instrument panel, and the steering wheel with three painted spokes and the blue oval on its hub.

DASHBOARD, INSTRUMENTS AND CONTROLS

There were no surprises associated with the Mk III's dashboard, and its layout was immediately familiar to anyone who knew the earlier Capris. Once again there were two-dial and six-dial versions; the latter is sometimes perversely called a "four-dial" type because of its four minor instruments. All dashboards had a full cut-out to enable a radio to be fitted (like that on the later Mk II models), and this was covered by a plastic panel if one was not.

From the start of Mk III production in 1978, all models had a "soft-feel" covering for the instrument panel and its padded surround, which was less stark in appearance than its Mk II equivalent. On all early models, this was black, although the S models always had a Chocolate-coloured dashboard when Chocolate trim was fitted. (A Chocolate-coloured dashboard was also used on the GT4 and Cameo special editions.) Grey dashboards arrived with the 2.8-litre cars in 1981, and then spread to other models as well.

All Mk III dashboards incorporated a drop-down glove box on the passenger's side, with its own lock and interior light. An ash tray in the centre of the dashboard was also standard from the beginning. The Ghia models were the only ones to have a grab handle on the passenger's side of the dashboard.

Dials, switches and warning lights

On the entry-level two-dial dashboard that was used on 1300, L and GL models, one dial is the speedometer and the other contains fuel and water temperature gauges. The six-dial dashboard was used for the S and Ghia models, and also for the LS and then the Laser models that were introduced in October 1984. On these, the water and temperature gauges are moved to the satellite locations, along with the oil pressure

The more expensive models had a steering wheel with trimmed spokes and centre section. Here it is on a Capri Laser.

CAPRI MK III DETAILS

The six-dial dashboard was combined with the bare-spoke steering wheel on the Capri Calypso, which also had red instrument bezels to give a distinctive character.

and battery condition indicators. The second large dial position is then used for a rev counter, of which there were two different types: these can be distinguished by a small number at the bottom of the dial, a 4 for a four-cylinder type, and a 6 for a six-cylinder rev counter.

The main dials are similar to those on the Mk II but have a number of differences. On the six-dial dashboard, both of them have red needles in place of the Mk II's white ones, but on the two-dial dashboard the speedometer needle is yellow. On the rev counter, numbers "10", "20", "30" and so on replace the "1000", "2000" and "3000" of the Mk II type, and on the speedometer the sub-markings for the kilometres-per-hour speeds are marked in white instead of yellow, while the dial reads (somewhat optimistically) to 140mph instead of 130mph. The speedometer on the S, LS and Ghia models has a trip meter, but there is none on the lower-specification cars. A special feature of the LS models (and of the Calypso editions) was red bezels for all six dials.

There are also several differences in the markings of the minor instruments on the six-dial dashboard, which are an ammeter and oil pressure gauge on the left, and a fuel gauge and coolant temperature gauge on the right. All dashboards incorporated a switch for the hazard warning light system from the start, and this was located below the instrument panel and outboard of the driver. A handbrake warning light was standard on GL models and above, and from April 1979 all dashboards gained a brake fluid level warning light.

As was by now traditional for the Capri, the radio (see below) was mounted in the centre of the dashboard, at the left-hand end of the instrument binnacle. Below this were the sliding switches for the heating and ventilating controls, with

This was the layout of the standard six-dial dashboard, with black instrument bezels against a black background. The instruments always had orange needles.

FACTORY-ORIGINAL FORD CAPRI MK II & MK III

A Ford-branded stereo radio-cassette head unit is seen in this 1986 Capri Laser. The arrangement of the four switches below the heater control panel is clear. The ash tray below it was a drop-down type.

Also Ford-branded, this is a different type of radio-cassette head unit, this time in a 1985 Capri Laser.

a two-speed booster fan, and underneath those were four switches. Reading from left to right, these were for the rear fog guard lights (with an amber telltale), the rear washer, the rear wiper, and the heated rear window (again with an amber telltale).

Radio

The entry-level 1.3-litre Capri did not have a radio as standard, and nor did the early L-specification models. Instead, there was a plastic cover panel over the aperture in the dashboard. However, a radio was standard on GL, S and Ghia models from the start of Mk III Capri production.

The changes to the standard radio specification during the production life of the Mk III Capri were both multiple and potentially confusing, and they are most easily understood from a table.

March 1978
Ford P32 push-button MW/LW mono
   Standard on GL, S and Ghia;
   extra-cost option for base 1.3 and L
Ford M21 MW/LW radio with manual tuning
   Extra-cost option for base 1.3 and L

April 1979
Ford P21 push-button radio   Standard on L
Ford RST 21P push-button radio with stereo cassette
   Standard on Ghia; extra-cost option for L, GS and S
Ford P32 MW/LW/VHF push-button radio
   Extra-cost option for L, GS and S
Ford SRT 32P MW/LW/VHF stereo radio with stereo cassette player
   Extra-cost option on all models,
   but cost less if ordered with the Ghia trim

August 1981
Ford P32 MW/LW/VHF push-button radio
   Standard on GL and S; extra-cost option for L and LS
Ford SRT 32P MW/LW/VHF stereo radio with stereo cassette player   Standard on Ghia

July 1982
Ford SRT 32P MW/LW/VHF stereo radio with stereo cassette player
   Standard on all 2.8-litre; always with an electric aerial

September 1983
Ford SRT 32P MW/LW/VHF stereo radio with stereo cassette player   Standard on 1.6 LS and 2.0 S

October 1984
Ford SRT 32P MW/LW/VHF stereo radio with stereo cassette player   Standard on Laser

The trimmed version of the steering wheel is seen here in a Capri Laser.

The speedometer was marked to a rather optimistic 140mph and incorporated a trip counter. Just visible at the bottom of the rev counter here is the tiny figure 4, denoting the instrument for a four-cylinder car.

as on the Mk II Capri. The ignition key itself normally had a ribbed black plastic grip, but from 1981 the LS models and above came with a "torch key", where the plastic grip contained a small light that made finding the ignition keylock in the dark considerably easier.

By this time, Ford had standardised the design of its control stalks across all of its European ranges. On the Capri, there were three as standard, one on the left of the steering column and two on the right. The left-hand one operates the horn, the turn signals and the headlamp flasher; the right-hand pair are for the main lighting and for the wipers, which have two speeds and an intermittent setting as well.

Steering wheel, column and stalk controls

There were five different types of Mk III steering wheel, and all of them had a blue Ford oval logo on the centre boss.

For all models except the Ghia, Ford initially standardised a 14-inch three-spoke steering wheel with a most attractive design. This was known as the "sports" steering wheel. Its rim was normally moulded in grey plastic to match the instrument panel, but there was a leather-trimmed version for the S models. A modified version of this three-spoke wheel became standard for the 1983 model-year, which was effectively the same wheel but with its metal spokes now concealed by grey plastic to match the rim. From October 1984, the 2.8 Injection Special and the Laser both had a variant of this later wheel with a leather-trimmed rim.

The early Ghia models retained the larger-diameter two-spoke steering wheel that had been used on the Mk II models. This steering wheel was also fitted on 3.0 S models if the power steering option was deleted to special order. Ghia models then took on the three-spoke "sports" steering wheel for the 1980 model-year.

A neat circular two-piece housing made of grey plastic conceals the steering column, and the key-operated ignition switch, which always incorporated an anti-theft lock for the steering column, is mounted in an outboard extension of it. The design of the housing, although not its colour, is the same

The untrimmed steering wheel was standard on the 3.0-litre Ghia model. Clear here is the grab handle on the passenger's side of the dash.

FACTORY-ORIGINAL FORD CAPRI MK II & MK III

All Mk III Capris had the same arrangement of steering column stalks, with one on the left and two on the right. These are seen in a 280 model.

The Quartz clock embedded in the centre console always had yellow hands, even though the main dials had red hands. This one is in a 1985 Capri Laser.

A rare option (strictly an accessory, as it could be had on other Fords of the time) for the Mk III Capris was the Speed Control system. Available by 1980, this was what is now generally called a cruise control, and was operated by an additional stalk on the right-hand side of the steering column. Wires apart, the other main evidence of its fitment was a vacuum-operated actuator unit in the engine bay.

Major controls

There were several different grips for the manual gear lever. L and GL models had a simple black grip with the shift gate marked on it in white. S and Ghia models had a "sports" grip, with leather trim, and this was also used on LS and Laser models. Five-speed cars had a different grip, borrowed from the Granada range, and this was trimmed in leather for the 2.8 Injection Special introduced in October 1984.

As on the Mk II Capris, the automatic gearbox selector has a black T-handle selector on a bright metal stalk. This operates in a straight gate within a domed console that is marked PRND21. The console is mounted to the flat section of the centre console when one is fitted, but on cars without one it is mounted directly to the transmission tunnel.

The pull-up handbrake is mounted between the front seats and has a plastic grip with a smooth top surface and ribbing on the underside. On all models except for the base 1300, it had a plastic "leatherette" gaiter, attached either to the transmission tunnel carpet or to the front of the stowage box housing on the centre console when one was fitted. On the 1300, there was a very basic black rubber gaiter attached to the transmission tunnel carpet.

The foot pedals all have the same style of black rubber pads with ribbing that runs from side to side.

INTERIOR TRIM

Centre console

From the start of Mk III production, GL models and above all had a centre console that incorporated a trinket tray and a quartz time clock at the dashboard end. This was also standard on all the 2.8-litre cars and on the LS. On the Ghia models, there was a storage compartment at the back of the trinket tray, between the seats, and this compartment had a padded centre armrest on top of it. From August 1981, this storage compartment and armrest also became standard on the GL models and above. With the arrival of the LS models, the centre console was given what Ford called "carpeted cowlside trim", which meant that the sides of the console and stowage box were carpeted to match the floor. This was then extended to all remaining production models.

This Capri Calypso is representative of the lower-specification cars, with no centre stowage box and no armrest between the seats.

CAPRI MK III DETAILS

The centre console and five-speed manual gear lever are pictured here in a 1986 Capri Laser model.

The centre console was designed to suit both manual and automatic gearchanges. Here it is with an automatic selector in a 3.0 Ghia model.

The more generous cut of the later leather handbrake gaiter is seen here on a Capri 280.

This was the basic type of door trim, with heat-moulded vinyl fronted by a "chrome" plastic strip. This one is seen on a 1981 Calypso.

Door trims, door seals and rear side trims

All door trim panels have the same overall design but on early cars there are several variations. All are trimmed in vinyl, which is normally black unless on a Ghia model, when the vinyl tones in with the upholstery colour.

On base 1300 models and on all L and early GL and S specification cars, the whole door card is trimmed in vinyl, with the moulded centre panel delineated by "chrome" plastic trim strips. At the top of the range, the Ghia models always had a carpeted lower section on the door trim, together with a velour centre panel that was delineated by the usual style of "chrome" plastic trim strips.

From August 1981, the GL models and above all had carpeted lower door panels, leaving only the cheaper models with all-vinyl trims. With the arrival of the 2.8-litre cars in 1981, the door trims were modified with a more obviously padded top section, and this style was carried over to the

The trim on this 1985 Laser is very different, with a central panel trimmed to match the upholstery, and a carpeted lower section.

The later models also had a different design of sill locking button. Without the bulbous top, it was almost impossible to pull up, which made it harder to break into the car. This is the 1985 Laser.

The door trim on this Ghia model is different yet again, with a centre panel that matches the upholstery, and a carpeted lower section. Note the toggle switch for the remote control door mirror, and the early type of sill locking button.

whole range for the 1983 model-year. There was also a change to the sill buttons in 1981, from the early mushroom-top type to a flush-fitting type that made it harder for a thief to open the door from outside after breaking a window. On the Laser models from October 1984, the basic colour of the door trim changed to grey, and there were centre panels in Truro fabric.

Release handles and window winders were generally made of black plastic, but the Ghia models had different types with a combination of bright metal and black plastic.

The rear quarter trims were designed to match the door trims, and were trimmed in the same way. None of them, however, had carpeted lower sections. All models had a black

This was the toggle control for the remote-control mirror on the driver's door.

Yet another variation on door trim design is seen here on a Capri 280, where the centre panel is perforated. The toggle control for the door mirror is all black, without the bright metal ring used on other models.

This is again a Laser, this time with dark grey trim and dating from 1986. The door trim once again has a cloth insert to match the upholstery, and there is a remote-control mirror.

CAPRI MK III DETAILS

Rear quarter trim panels followed the pattern of the door cards, and featured a swivelling ash tray as standard. This example is a basic type, on the 1981 Calypso.

This was the typical headlining of a Mk III Capri, with perforated vinyl material in an off-white or beige colour. This car, a 1985 Laser, is fitted with a sunroof. Note how its trim panel differs from that on Mk II cars, where a seam was always visible. Also clear here are the padded sun visors and the winding handle that operated the sunroof.

ash tray, which was let into the centre section of the trim or, on Ghia models, was mounted rather higher up to make room for an arm rest.

Headlining, sun visors and interior mirror

Head linings were made of washable vinyl with perforations, and on most models had an oatmeal colour. However, the 2.8 Injection models had a black headlining, and the 2.8 Injection Special had a headlining in Shark Grey to match the seat bolsters. The sun visors are trimmed to match on all models, although their coverings have no perforations, and there is a vanity mirror on the reverse of the passenger's side visor. There is a single courtesy light, located over the passenger's side door next to a black grab handle. When a sunroof is fitted, the underside of the sliding section is trimmed to match the headlining, and there is a manual winding handle that is recessed in a plastic housing just behind the rear-view mirror.

That rear-view mirror is mounted to a plinth on the windscreen header rail, and all models had a dipping type as standard from the start of production in 1978.

Rear parcels shelf

The Mk III was the only Capri variant to have a proper parcels shelf – "package tray" in Ford-speak. This is a moulded fibreboard item, which has become quite rare in good condition because it disintegrates after absorbing condensation over long periods of time.

There was a non-slip carpet material inserted into the panels of this tray. The carpet was normally black or grey, but on Ghia models the inserts matched the colour of the interior. The tray has a black nylon cord at each end to attach it to the underside of the hatchback, so that the shelf will lift up to give good access to the boot when the hatchback is open. These cords can be detached from the hatchback if the shelf has to

The removable rear parcels shelf is seen here on a Ghia model, where the recesses of the shelf are trimmed to match the interior colour. There is a black rubber seal on the edge nearest to the camera, which acts as a buffer to prevent rattles. The cables that raise the shelf with the hatchback have been detached here, and are hanging down through the shelf.

This is the shelf in a 1981 Calypso, showing the type of carpeting then in use for the recesses. There is some damage to this shelf (a row of holes running front to back on each side), and the ICE speakers visible are aftermarket additions.

A different type of carpet material was in use by the time of this 1985 Laser model. In this case, the cables have been laid out neatly on the shelf itself.

Yet another type of carpet infill is seen here, this time with a more block-like pattern. This is a very late Capri 280.

be removed from the car.

This parcels shelf was standard on GL, S and Ghia models from the start of production, but was initially an extra-cost item on the base 1300 cars and on the L trim derivatives. Then from January 1981, the parcels shelf was made standard across the range.

Carpets and flooring

There were three grades of carpet for the passenger cabin. A very basic, non-woven, type was standard on early models and was later used for the LS models as well. Ghia models always had a shag-pile carpet – Ford called it a "deep velour" type – and then from August 1981 a cut-pile type was used on the GL models (but not on the L or the LS); it was then standardised on the 2.0 S as well in March 1983. The carpets in the early S models were very thin, and from the start of the 1980 model-year these models benefited from additional sound insulation under the carpets. This additional insulation was also made standard on the 2.8-litre cars from the start of their production in 1981.

All carpets are "fitted", which means they consist of a single section that is cut to shape. All of them also have a plastic heel mat for the driver that is sewn to the relevant area. As the transmission tunnel differs between manual and automatic models, there are corresponding differences between the carpets.

SEATS, UPHOLSTERY AND SEAT BELTS

The story of the seat and upholstery types used in the Mk III Capri is a very complicated one, and this section therefore makes use of a table to explain that story. Upholstery types are discussed after the section on front seat types, but of course rear seats always shared the upholstery style applied to the front seats.

Rear seats

The rear seat backrest always folded forwards to allow the load space to be enlarged. On the entry-level 1300 models, this backrest was a single piece, but on all other models it was split into two equal sections, which allowed more flexible use of the load area. There were never any headrests for the rear seats.

Seat belts

Inertia-reel front safety belts were standard on all models from the start of production. Note that the lower mountings for the front seat belts changed in autumn 1980 (see the earlier section on Floorpan and Sills), and the belts themselves changed to suit.

No rear belts were fitted as standard, but a pair of lap-and-diagonal inertia-reel belts could be had at extra cost from the start. These became standard on Ghia models from January 1981 and standard on both Laser and 2.8 Injection Special models from August 1986.

CAPRI MK III DETAILS

These two pictures of the seats in the 1981 Capri Calypso show the configuration of the basic seats in the Mk III range. The striped cloth upholstery was nevertheless special to the Calypso.

This is a front seat headrest from the Calypso, again representing the basic Mk III specification.

FACTORY-ORIGINAL FORD CAPRI MK II & MK III

FRONT SEATS

Seven different designs of front seat were used in the Mk III Capri.
In all cases, the backrests tipped forwards to give access to the rear seats.
   The seven seat types were as follows:

Fixed backrest, no head rest	(1978- 1980)
Reclining backrest, no head rest	(1978-1983)
Roll-top	(1978-1981)
(Recliner with head rest that retracted fully into the seat back)	
Recaro with "net" head rest	(1978-1981)
(Headrest is a frame with net across it)	
Recaro with solid head rest	(1981-1986)
(Front seat back has Recaro tag)	
Escort type, with solid head rest	(1982-1984)
(First introduced in the Escort XR3)	
Reclining backrest, with solid head rest	(1981-1986)
(First introduced in the Escort GL)	

FRONT SEATS AND UPHOLSTERY COMBINATIONS

The simplest way of explaining Ford's use of the different seat and upholstery types is by this table. Note that the special-edition types are not covered here; details will be found in the tables on page 102.

Model	Date	Seat style	Upholstery
1300	1978	Fixed	Beta Plus
		No options	
L	1978-1980	Fixed	Concord
		Roll-top optional	
	1980 (May)	Reclining, no head rest	Concord
	1981 (Feb)	Reclining, no head rest	Sandford
GL	1978	Fixed	Diamond
		Roll-top optional	
	1979 (Oct)	Reclining, with head rest	Windsor
	1982-1983	Reclining, with head rest	York
S	1978	Roll-top	
		Recaro with "net" headrest optional	Carla
	1981 (summer)	Recaro with solid headrest standard	Carla
			Laser in late 1982
	1983 (Jan)	Escort type	Laser
LS	1981	Reclining, with head rest	Carla
		Roll-top optional	
	1983	Reclining, with head rest	Laser
Ghia	1978	Roll-top	Verona
Laser	1984 (Oct)	Reclining, with head rest	Truro II
2.8	1981	Recaro with solid headrest	Carla
	1983		Monza
2.8 Inj			
Spl	1984	Recaro with solid headrest	Strobe
280	1986	Recaro with solid headrest	Raven leather

These seats in a 1985 Laser model show the Truro II fabric with its herringbone pattern for the wearing surfaces.

The front seat backrests were released by the lever visible here on the side, in order to give access to the rear seats.

These seats had a turnwheel adjustment for the backrest rake.

The Diamond upholstery is seen here in a Cameo special edition.

UPHOLSTERY

The whole picture was complicated by the multiple changes of upholstery type over the years. For details of the colours available, please see the Paints and Trims table on page 71; what follows is an overview of the different types and their characteristics.

Beta Plus fabric
This was a plain fabric used on entry-level 1300 models only.

Carla fabric
This was a bold tartan fabric used for the centre panels of seat cushions and backrests of the S models between 1978 and May 1982. It was also used for the LS models from February 1981 to May 1982, and then again from May 1983 until they were replaced by the Laser models in October 1984.

On the S models, Carla fabric was paired with black Savannah plain fabric on the bolsters and seat backs. On the LS, and on the early 2.8 Injection cars, it was paired with grey crushed velour for the bolsters and backs of the seats.

Concord fabric
This was a check fabric used on the centre panels of seat cushions and backrests of the L models between 1978 and 1981. Each square of the check had four round dots within it. Concord was paired with Savannah plain fabric on the backs of the seats.

Diamond fabric
This was a patterned, single-colour fabric used on GL models between 1978 and 1979 only.

Laser fabric
This was a black fabric with bold grey or red stripes running from side to side. There was also a version with red stripes. It was used on the Recaro seats of S models from May 1982 until S production ended in September 1984 and on those of LS models from May 1982 until May 1983.

Monza fabric
This perforated grey cloth was used only for the 2.8-litre models from January 1983, when it was paired with darker grey crushed velour bolsters.

Raven leather
The only standard production models to have full leather trim were the very late Capri 280 models based on the 2.8 Injection Special.

Sandford fabric
This was a single-colour fabric with a large square pattern in the weave. It was used for the seat facings of L models from February 1981 and replaced Concord fabric.

Strobe fabric
Strobe fabric was a black and grey fabric used for the centre panels of seat cushions and backrests on 2.8 Injection Special models from October 1984. It always came with grey leather bolsters and is often called the "half-leather" type. Leather was also used for the backs of the seats.

Truro II fabric
This was a grey herringbone fabric with stripes woven into it, and was used only in the Laser models from October 1984.

Verona fabric
This was a single-colour fabric used for the seat facings of all Mk III Ghia models.

Windsor fabric
This was a single-colour fabric that replaced Diamond fabric on GL models in October 1979 for the 1980 model-year. It was replaced by York fabric from May 1982.

York fabric
This was a single-colour fabric that replaced Windsor fabric on GL models in May 1982.

These are the early type of Ghia seats, with Verona fabric upholstery. The whole style of the seat, with built-in front head restraints, is quite different from that of later Mk III models.

This 1978 launch publicity picture shows the Carla check fabric used in the S models, with the optional Recaro front seats which had headrests with net centre sections.

CAPRI MK III DETAILS

Recaro seats with shaped bolsters were available on the 2.8-litre models. These ones have the perforated leather that was an option for the final 280 models.

FACTORY-ORIGINAL FORD CAPRI MK II & MK III

The Monza upholstery on the early 2.8-litre cars is sometimes described as the velour type, for reasons that will be obvious from this picture. The more obviously padded style of door card that was first seen on these models is also visible in this picture.

With the carpet removed, the hardboard boot floor was revealed.

Boot interior

As was familiar Capri practice, the spare wheel was stowed underneath a lift-out boot floor. To suit the wider spare tyre of the 2.8-litre cars, this false floor was mounted an inch higher than in other models.

The boot floor had a rubber mat in the entry-level 1300 models, and also on the Cameo special edition. On all other models there was a removable carpet section, although

Underneath the boot floor were the fuel tank, spare wheel, rear washer reservoir and pump, and the wheel-changing tools.

this was made of the same black material regardless of whether the passenger compartment had cut-pile or shag-pile carpeting.

A luggage compartment light was always standard on GL and Ghia models, and was also standard on the LS and 2.8-litre cars from the start of their production in 1981. The S models nevertheless did not have one before January 1983, when it became standard.

Spare wheel well and tools

The underfloor stowage arrangements are the same as on the Mk II models, and the boot floor lifts out to provide access. The largest item on view is the spare wheel, which lies flat in a recess offset towards the left of the car. To its

Velour carpet was used for the floor of the boot in Ghia models. Also visible here is one of the boot lights, embedded in the moulded plastic trim that covers the inner rear wheelarch.

CAPRI MK III DETAILS

The underside of the removable boot floor is seen here in a 1985 Capri Laser. The simple location fixing at the front edge is clearly visible. The sticker on the left shows the body colour and its code.

Not all boot floors were the same! This one belongs to a Capri 280, one of the final production models, and quite clearly has an additional locating lip around its edges.

The boot carpet on lower-specification models is made of a quite different material. There are nevertheless colour variations: the darker grey here is on a Capri Calypso, and the lighter one on a Capri Laser. The plastic side trims were always black, even though the right-hand one in the Laser looks blue in the picture.

Yet another variation of the underfloor scene. This is a Capri Calypso, and most obviously has a suppressor attached to the wiring running across the forward edge of the spare wheel well. There are no boot lights on the plastic wheelarch covers, as was the case with all lower-specification models.

left, and just inside the tail panel, is the translucent plastic reservoir for the rear window washer. The washer pump is located on the same side but in front of the wheel.

The wheel-changing tools are mounted on the right of the underfloor compartment, with the screw-type jack held against the tail panel by a pair of plastic cords. Most jacks appear to have been black. Also secured by those plastic cords is the wheelnut wrench. This was always black up to summer 1982, and then the 1983 and later models had a silver one which had a wedge-shaped red plastic end. This wedge was designed to aid removal of the wheel trims on other Ford models such as Sierras, and was of no use to Capri owners.

FACTORY-ORIGINAL FORD CAPRI MK II & MK III

SPECIAL EDITIONS AND SPECIAL OPTIONS

There were several special editions of the Mk III in the early 1980s, when they were needed to support flagging Capri sales. As noted elsewhere, the Laser was marketed as a special edition between June and October 1984, after which it became a mainstream trim level.

There was no doubting the identity of the Capri Calypso, which carried its name in a large decal on the tailgate.

The GT4 edition, 1980

The GT4 was the first special-edition Capri Mk III, and was introduced in March 1980. The base model was a Capri 1.6 L, and just 500 examples were built. All of them had black painted windscreen pillars, three graduated decals on the nose of the bonnet, and matching side decals.

The GT4 was available in three colours: Diamond White (with Dark Red decals), Signal Red '80 (with Dark Brown decals) or Strato Silver (with Dark Green decals). Upholstery was always Beta Plus fabric upholstery in Bitter Chocolate. The model's special features included head restraints, a six-dial dashboard with red bezels for the dials, two door mirrors, a rear wiper and a rear parcels shelf. Just three of these attractive cars were known to survive at the time of writing.

The Cameo edition, 1981

This was a budget special edition introduced in July 1981. It was based on a 1.3 L or 1.6 L, and the cost savings were made by deleting the rear parcels shelf, the clock and the centre console. Only eight paint colours, none of them metallics, were available:

Paint	Interior colour
Diamond White	Blue or Chocoloate
Dove Grey	Chocolate or Tan
Meadow Green	Chocolate or Tan
Midnight Blue	Blue or Tan
Prairie Yellow	Chocolate or Tan
Terracotta	Chocolate or Tan
Tuscan Beige	Chocolate or Tan
Venetian Red	Chocolate or Tan

Cameos all had a contrasting two-colour lower side stripe decal, in one of four colour combinations:
Dark Brown and Orange
Medium Blue and Light Blue
Medium Green and Light Green
Red and Orange

The body side decals were in either Argent and Blue or Argent and Red.

The GT4 was the first of the Capri Mk III special editions, and had some very distinctive decals. The car in the background of this Ford publicity picture is one of the Zakspeed racing Capris, prepared in Germany.

The Tempo edition

The Tempo edition was another budget model, based on the 1.3 or 1.6 Capri and introduced in August 1981. These cars were not built as Tempos but were turned into Tempos by Ford dealers, and are said to have been created as a way of selling low-specification old-model cars in unpopular colours. They are now extremely rare.

Tempos normally had steel wheels with 5-inch rims and 165 x 13 tyres; alloy wheels with 185/70 tyres were optional. There were no exterior side mouldings, and the cabin had no centre console.

The Calypso edition

The Calypso special edition was also introduced in July 1981, but in this case added features to the mid-range 1.6 LS model. It came with two-tone paint, tinted windows, and a rear wash-wipe, plus steel sports wheels. The interior featured Laser upholstery. An extra-cost option pack was also available, adding a sunroof, opening rear quarter-lights and a remotely operated driver's door mirror. Just five colour combinations were available, as follows:

Cardinal Red over Strato Silver
Crystal Green over Strato Silver
Forest Green over Crystal Green
Graphite Grey over Strato Silver
Titan Blue over Strato Silver.

In each case, there was a dark grey decal strip on the sides of the car, just below the boundary between the two colours. None of the cars appear to have carried any Calypso identification.

The Cabaret edition

The Cabaret edition was introduced in May 1982 and was based on the 1.6 L model, although a 2.0-litre version could also be ordered. It was distinguished on the outside by decal stripes, a sunroof, a rear spoiler and 5.5-inch steel sports wheels. Inside the cabin, the additions were a six-dial dashboard, a centre console, grey Sanford cloth upholstery with grey or blue Ascot cloth inserts, cut-pile carpet, and Ghia-style door trims.

The Cabaret was available in four solid and six metallic colours:

Solids
Black   Caribbean Blue
Cardinal Red   Diamond White

Metallics
Champagne Gold   Graphite Grey
Crystal Green   Strato Silver
Forest Green   Titan Blue

The first version of the Capri Cabaret shows off its distinctive graphics. This example is in Strato Silver with upper body decals in Argent and Blue. The wheels are the 5.5-inch version of the sports type, as seen on GL models.

The Cabaret II special edition had clear identification at the rear.

FACTORY-ORIGINAL FORD CAPRI MK II & MK III

The Calypso and Cabaret models are seen here in a page from a May 1982 sales brochure.

There was a single thick coachline on the Capri Calypso, just below the boundary between the two paint colours.

The Calypso II edition

The Calypso II edition capitalised on the success of the earlier Calypso edition and was introduced approximately a year later, in May 1982. The base model was a 1.6-litre with steel sports wheels, and the key selling point was once again the two-tone paintwork. This could be had in three combinations:

Cardinal Red over Strato Silver
Forest Green over Strato Silver
Graphite Grey over Strato Silver

All cars appear to have had a Calypso decal on the hatchback, next to the "Capri 1.6" decal. Two door mirrors were standard, and the seats were Capri S-type Recaros with net head rests, upholstered in Carla cloth, while the six-dial dashboard had red instrument bezels. Confusingly, the sales brochure described the car simply as a Calypso rather than a Calypso II!

The Cabaret II edition

The original Cabaret edition proved popular, and so Ford repeated the trick in January 1983 with the Cabaret II model. The base model was a 1.6 L or a 2.0 L. Exterior features were a sunroof, opening rear side windows, a rear spoiler, 185/70 tyres, a locking filler cap, an electric aerial for the stereo ICE system, and a Cabaret motif on the tailgate. Interior features were Recaro reclining front seats with head restraints, revised trim, a centre armrest, and a torch key. These cars had tinted glass, a rear wash-wipe system, LS-style seats and a radio-cassette as well. All of them had the four-speed gearbox.

The Cabaret II special edition was available only in three two-tone metallic combinations:

Caspian Blue over Glacier Blue
Caspian Blue over Strato Silver
Imperial Red over Strato Silver

There were two lower body side stripe options: Red over Blue or Blue over Red.

The Capri 280

The Capri 280 was also known as the Brooklands after its Brooklands Green metallic paint. These were the last Capris to be built, and a total of 1038 were made in Cologne in December 1986. They went on sale in Britain in March 1987 and the last one was sold towards the end of the year. They had coachlines that incorporated a 280 motif, and 15-inch alloy wheels with low-profile tyres. The interior featured Recaro front seats, leather upholstery (known as Raven) with burgundy piping, leather on the steering wheel rim and shift grip, and a self-seeking radio-cassette unit.

These cars had a decal badge on the left of the tail, reading "Capri 280" in Dark Red and White, and decal side stripes in White over Mid Red. All of them had the five-speed manual gearbox.

CAPRI MK III DETAILS

THE X PACK

The Capri X-Pack was a menu of performance and handling improvements for the 3.0-litre cars that was carried over from the Mk II Capri. However, it appears not to have been actively promoted for the Mk III models before autumn 1980. It was not available direct from the showrooms but the chosen elements could be added to an existing car by one of the authorised Fordsport dealers. It was, therefore, strictly a Ford-approved conversion that used Ford-developed parts. It was also expensive, which ensured that X-Pack cars were few and far between, and as the precise specification of an X-Pack car depended on the buyer, it is likely that no two cars were exactly alike.

Central to the X-Pack was an uprated 3.0-litre V6 engine, delivering 175bhp at 5000rpm and 194 lb ft of torque at 4000rpm while retaining the standard compression ratio.

The X-Pack – or Series X as it is called in this publicity picture – had several optional components. This car is a Capri S with the special front and rear spoilers.

This engine had a new inlet manifold with three twin-choke Weber 42DCNF carburettors and a special air cleaner; the inlet valves were 17% larger than standard and the exhaust valves 22% larger. There were special head gaskets and an electronic ignition system, plus a high-capacity radiator and a free-flow exhaust system.

There was a chassis package as well, with front springs stiffened by 38%, a modified and stiffened anti-roll bar, and the front struts were relocated to give better steering response from increased negative camber. Bilstein gas dampers were fitted all round, and there were new ventilated front brake discs with a larger diameter than standard. There was a limited-slip differential option.

Wheels could have either 7-inch or 7.5-inch rims, the latter running on 205/60 VR 13 tyres. With the 7.5-inch wheels, it was necessary to fit wing extensions. These were made of GRP, were made by Zakspeed in Germany, and were both bonded and riveted to the bodyshell.

This 1980 car goes a step further, with the deep-dish wheels, wide wings and special side decals as well.

FACTORY-ORIGINAL FORD CAPRI MK II & MK III

AFTERMARKET SPECIALS

The "performance" image of the Capri continued to attract aftermarket companies when the Mk II and Mk III models were in production. Turbocharging became a popular way of getting extra performance during the 1970s and remained so during the 1980s. There were several aftermarket conversions available, although in Britain the one most fondly remembered is the Tickford Turbo, based on the Mk III and probably best described as a semi-official conversion on the grounds that it had Ford approval and was sold through Ford dealers.

These two pictures show a prototype iteration of the Tickford car, which here wears a "2.8 T" decal badge on the rear. Although the basic specification of the production car was in place, many items would alter; the badges and the wheel trims are among the most obvious.

BODYKITS

The 1980s was the era of the bodykit – a series of supposedly aerodynamic additions which equally supposedly aided performance. Most of these bodykits consisted of various combinations of specially shaped sill panels and spoilers; there was usually a front apron spoiler, plus a rear spoiler that mounted on the hatchback, and in some cases a rear apron diffuser was available as well. The truth was that most of these bodykits were intended more for show than for go, and that some of them were quite poorly made.

Perhaps the best known of the bodykits made for the Mk II and Mk III Capris were those from Richard Grant, which were widely available in accessory shops. Further up the market, Janspeed offered a kit for the 2.8 Injection models that consisted of a front spoiler, a rear bib spoiler, a "Cologne" rear wing spoiler, and side skirts.

JANSPEED

Janspeed were based at Salisbury in Wiltshire and could supply a wide range of tuning accessories for the Mk II and Mk III Capris. The company was always best known for its turbocharger conversions but it also supplied special exhaust manifolds and systems, modified cylinder heads, performance camshafts, twin-Weber carburettor conversions (for the Pinto engines), and uprated suspension with appropriate wheel and tyre combinations. Typically, the company would carry out the performance modifications itself, but most items were also available individually for installation by a competent owner.

By the time of the Mk II Capri, Janspeed was offering two turbocharger conversions; one was for the 3.0-litre V6 engine and the other for the 1.6-litre Pinto. Later on, conversions were also made available for the 2.0-litre Pinto engine and then the 2.8-litre V6 as well. Janspeed favoured Roto-Master turbochargers for all its conversions.

The Janspeed conversion for the Pinto engines had a single turbocharger that was arranged to suck through an SU carburettor. The compression ratio was lowered to

AFTERMARKET SPECIALS

This was the production reality. The swoops of the special lower panels (too good to be described as a "bodykit"!) are very apparent in this dead side view.

prevent detonation by means of a compression plate, and turbo boost was limited to 7psi by a wastegate. A simple crossover pipe linked the turbocharger's compressor turbine to the standard inlet manifold, and there was also a pipe between the turbocharger and the sump, to drain oil from the turbocharger bearing. Janspeed claimed that their turbocharger conversion gave power and torque gains of around 30% on a 1.6-litre engine, and it would be reasonable to assume that the turbocharged 2.0-litre Pinto conversion gave similar results.

The turbocharged 3.0-litre engines again had a single turbocharger, in this case mounted directly on top of the left-hand cylinder bank and providing 5psi of boost to give around 172bhp. The Weber carburettor was re-jetted and the cylinder heads had to be modified to lower the compression ratio and prevent detonation. When Janspeed did the conversion themselves, they normally fitted an oil cooler, a full custom exhaust system with low back pressure, and a boost gauge on the dashboard.

There is a story that Ford in Britain planned to mark the end of 3.0-litre V6 production in 1981 with a special edition that featured the Janspeed turbocharged conversion, and it appears that four evaluation cars were built. However, the plan for a turbocharged special edition was abandoned when the 2.8-litre cars became available.

Later, Janspeed also developed a turbocharger conversion to suit the 2.8-litre V6-engined Mk III models. Janspeed supposedly supplied around 80 conversion kits in all.

TURBO TECHNICS CAPRI

Turbo Technics was a Northampton-based company which developed an expertise in aftermarket turbocharger conversions during the 1980s. From July 1986, its neat turbocharged conversion of the Capri 2.8 Injection model was made available through selected Ford dealers in Britain.

The engine delivered 200bhp at 5500rpm with 247 lb ft of torque at 3800rpm, and the suspension and brakes were uprated to suit.

The Turbo Technics Capri was claimed to deliver 0-60mph in 6.5 seconds and a top speed of 143mph.

THE BROADSPEED CONVERSIONS

Ralph Broad's Broadspeed tuning company was based at Southam in Warwickshire, and developed a formidable road-going turbocharged conversion of the 3.0-litre V6 Mk I Capri that was known as the Broadspeed Bullit (the name and spelling were inspired by the 1968 film *Bullitt*, in which Steve McQueen memorably drove a Ford Mustang in a high-speed street chase). This conversion remained available during the Capri Mk II era, but the Capri Mk II Register knows of only five cars that were converted, and of only two that still existed at the time of publication.

The Broadspeed conversions were only ever available as complete cars, and not as kits of parts to be fitted by the

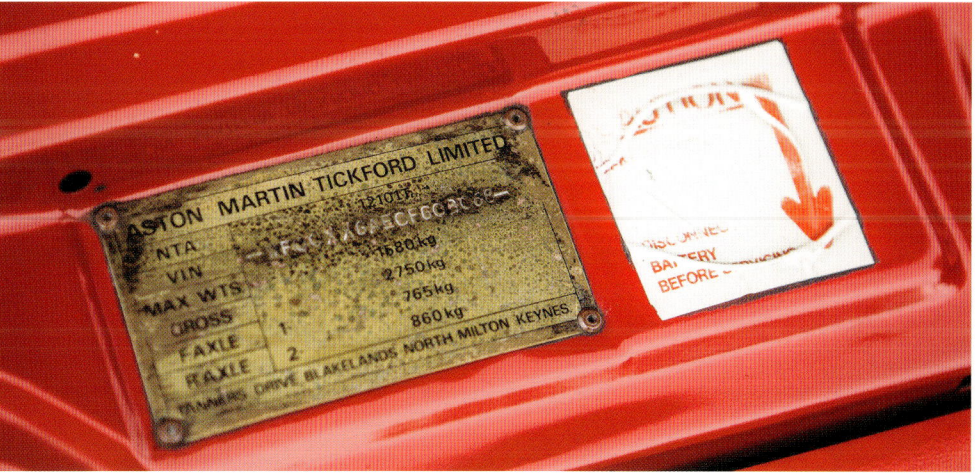

The Tickford cars had various types of identification plate. This one shows the maker's name as Aston Martin Tickford Ltd.

owner. As they were built to individual order, it is likely that no two were exactly alike. The 3.0-litre engines had a single re-jetted carburettor enclosed in a pressurised box, and the turbocharger was arranged to blow through it. The compression ratio was lowered to avoid detonation problems and there were modifications to the inlet and exhaust manifolds, and to the cylinder heads. A high-lift camshaft was fitted, and the whole rotating assembly was blueprinted. The cars came with handling modifications and body addenda (such as a front spoiler), as well as uprated suspension. A Broadspeed Bullit based on a Mk II Capri was capable of at least 125mph, with enhanced acceleration to match.

THE JEFF UREN STAMPEDE

Jeff Uren's tuning business was called Race Proved Performance and Equipment Ltd, was based at Ashburton in Devon, and was famous for high-performance Ford conversions that included the Capri Comanche. This was based on a 3.0-litre V6 Mk I and had four different states of tune, the most powerful being a triple-carburettor 218bhp type.

Uren also offered a Capri conversion with the 302 cubic-inch (5.0-litre) V8 from the US-built Ford Mustang, and this model was known as the Stampede. Wheel and brake modifications were a part of the package. The Stampede was first announced in 1972 but remained available as a conversion into the era of the Capri Mk II. Build quantities are not known for certain, but there were probably very few Stampede conversions of the Mk II Capri because Jeff Uren closed his business at the end of the 1970s. A reasonable estimate would be that four cars were built, but only one is known for certain to survive.

THE TICKFORD TURBO

The Tickford Turbo was a high-performance derivative of the Mk III Capri that was constructed with a degree of official co-operation. It was originally planned as a full Ford-approved conversion, but its key supporter at Ford of Europe, Bob Lutz, was promoted to a more senior position at Ford in the USA as development progressed, and so the major responsibility then fell onto Tickford. Although it had started life as a coachbuilding company, at that stage Tickford was owned by Aston Martin and was operating as a bespoke conversions company that primarily worked on projects for major manufacturers.

Aston Martin developed the mechanical elements of the Tickford Turbo with assistance from Ford SVE at Dunton, and the associated bodykit came from Aston Martin's chief stylist, Simon Saunders. There was also input from Capri racer John Miles, who had specialised in suspension work on the cars. Some development work was outsourced to Dave Cook Racing.

The Tickford Turbo was shown as a concept at the NEC Motor Show in October 1982. Production began in 1983 and the plan was to build a total of 100 cars, although some sources claim that no more than 86 were actually completed, the last of them in 1987. The first Tickfords were converted from 2.8i models, but later ones were based on the 2.8 Injection Special. All Tickford Turbos were capable of 140mph, with a 0-60mph time of 6.0 seconds. Mid-range acceleration was also extremely rapid, the 50-70mph increment taking 3.8 seconds and 50-80mph taking 4.4 seconds.

The Tickford cars started life as 2.8-litre Capris in Germany, and were shipped to the Aston Martin Tickford facility in Britain. Here, they were stripped down and then built up with the Tickford Turbo specification by hand. This was a very time-consuming and costly operation which meant that the finished cost of a Tickford Capri was nearly three times that of the original car – a fact which ensured exclusivity, if nothing else.

Much of the information that follows has been sourced from the web site www.a400mod.com, and readers with a special interest in the Tickford Capri should visit that.

Identification

Tickford Capris have a special brass VIN plate which is attached to the bonnet slam panel by rivets in the same way as a standard Capri plate. Some of these plates give the maker's name as Aston Martin Tickford Ltd, but others show the manufacturer as Ford. The VIN is unaltered from that of the host Capri.

Bodyshell

The standard Capri bodyshell is modified by the addition of a kit of GRP aerodynamic panels. In place of the standard grille is a plain panel painted to match the body, and below

The standard Capri grille was replaced by a flat panel with an indentation in the centre for the Ford oval, although on later cars this was replaced by other badges. The special front apron spoiler is also clear here.

AFTERMARKET SPECIALS

The bodykit of the Tickford cars remained unique to them. These pictures show how the black rubber bump-strip was used to conceal the join between bodykit and steel bodywork.

that is a deep front bumper and apron spoiler panel, with a letter-box air intake in the centre. There are chiselled side skirts at sill level, and a shaped rear bumper cover and valance. There is also a unique tail spoiler. (Note that the prototype car had flush wheel trims and an undertray, but neither featured on the production cars.)

Two further changes were made to the standard body. The bonnet profile was subtly modified to blend in with the blanking panel where the grille normally went, and there was an extra rubber door seal around the top of the front window frames to reduce wind noise at speeds over 100mph.

Badges

There were several varieties of badging, and it is probably impossible to be certain which one is original to any

There was a Tickford badge just below the indicator repeater on each front wing.

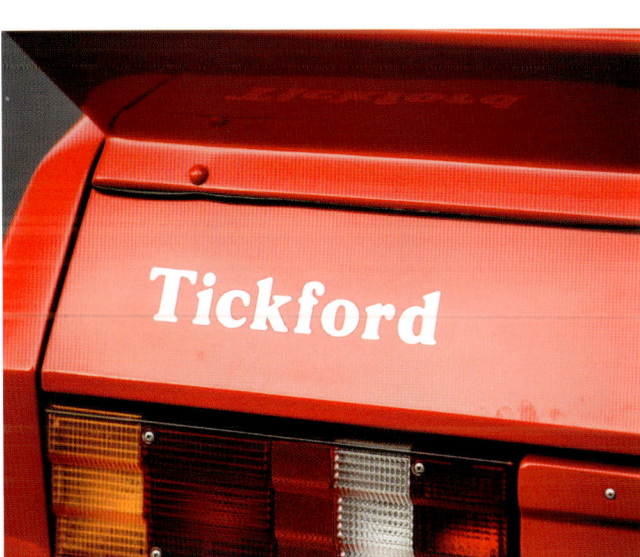

The Tickford cars had their own special identification arrangements at the rear.

Most obvious in this picture of a Tickford Turbo's boot is the special battery box on the left. The velour boot carpet was also unique to the model.

Extra sound deadening under the bonnet of the Tickford Capri was accompanied by a heat shield above the turbocharger. This picture also shows the shape of the special moulding around the headlights, normally concealed when the bonnet is closed.

individual car without photographic evidence. When Ford stopped promoting the car through their dealers in 1984, the Ford badges disappeared, and then when Tickford became independent of Aston Martin the Aston Martin badges disappeared. However, there seems to have been little consistency and there were doubtless anomalies.

All cars had an oval indentation in the centre of the grille blanking panel, into which on early cars a Ford oval badge was fitted. The Tickford Capri also had rectangular metal badges on each front wing and on the right-hand side of the rear hatch, enamelled in black with the Tickford name and the Aston Martin winged logo. There was also a decal badge on the left of the hatch, reading "Tickford Capri" in a Bookman Old Style font.

When Ford withdrew from the project in 1984, the Ford oval at the front was replaced by a Tickford wing emblem, similar to the Aston Martin logo but with a large T in the centre. The Tickford name was also added to the left-hand side of the front spoiler as a decal in Script font. At the same time, the three metal plate badges changed to feature the Tickford winged emblem instead of the Aston Martin type. The "Tickford Turbo" decal on the left of the rear hatch changed to a Script font to match that on the front spoiler.

Paints

The popular conception is that all the Tickford Capris were white with red coachlines, but in practice Tickford offered a choice of three colours – white, black or red. The 1984 Motor Show car had a pearlescent white finish, which was listed as an option for a huge £3262, and then pearlescent paint became standard in December 1986. For rather less (£2658), customers could order any colour they wanted, and as a result there were a few cars in what might be called "non-standard" finishes.

Electrical

The battery was relocated on the left-hand side of the boot to make room for all the additional equipment under the bonnet. A new main battery cable ran to the front of the car from the boot along the left-hand side of the transmission tunnel, and was clipped to it.

Central locking and electric windows were both standard on the Tickford Capri. Remote central locking and an automatic alarm system became standard on the very last cars, from December 1986. An optional Electric Pack brought power-adjustable door mirrors (made by Vitaloni in Italy) and a delay for the rear wiper system. Also available were double-dipping Cibie headlights.

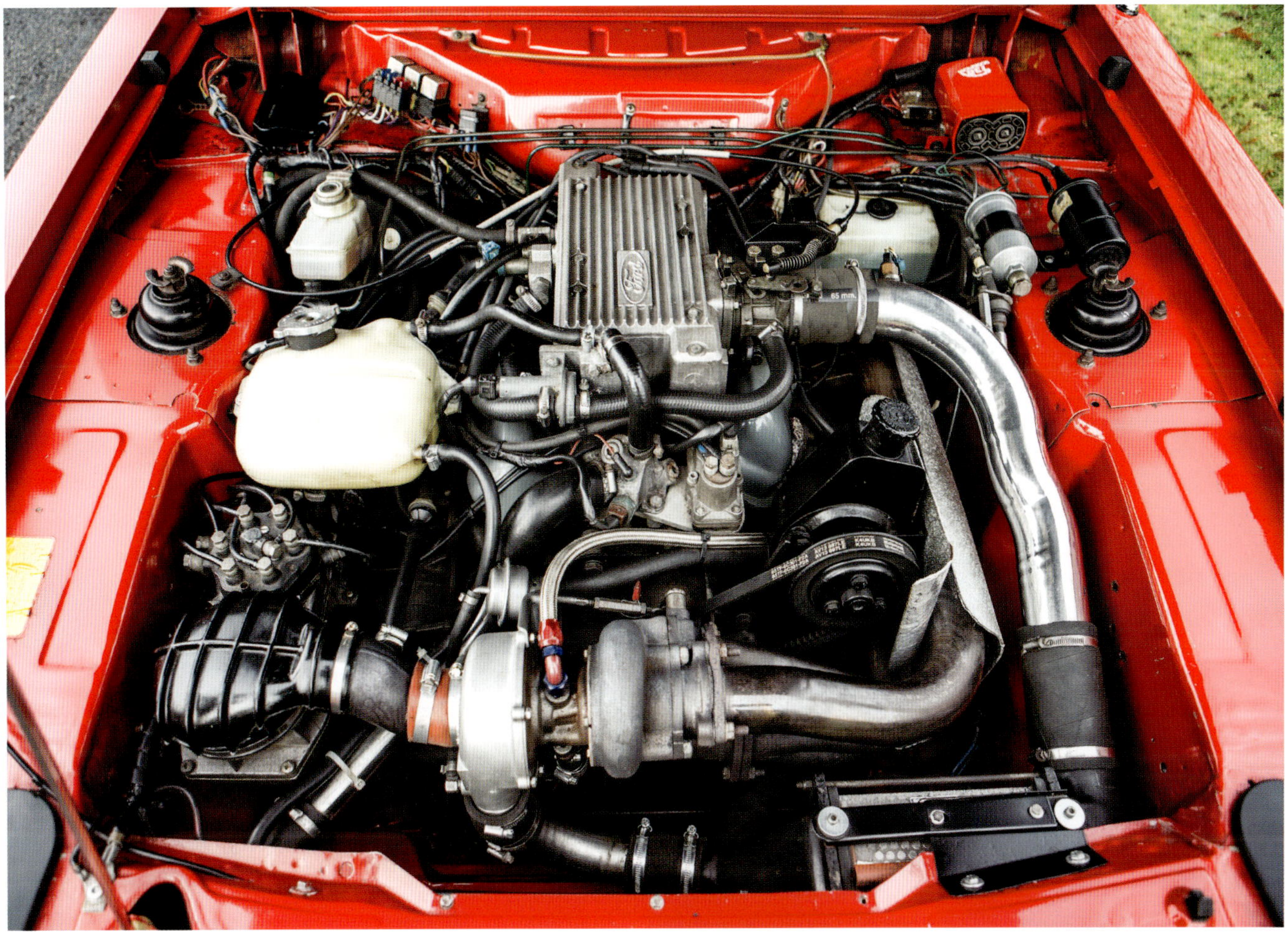

AFTERMARKET SPECIALS

There is simply no mistaking that underbonnet view, with the turbocharger right at the front of the engine bay. The turbocharger and its plumbing were very neatly installed – arguably showing up the lesser attention to detail elsewhere under the bonnet!

Engine, fuel system and exhaust

The base engine is a 2.8-litre Cologne V6, with performance boosted by a turbocharger and intercooler. Power was 205bhp at 5500rpm and torque was 260 lb ft at 3500rpm. The positions of several engine bay components had to be changed to make room for the additional items.

The turbocharger was an IHI type RHB6, mounted right at the front of the engine bay. Cold charge air came from a Garrett AiResearch intercooler and the engine retained the standard 9.2:1 compression pistons to minimise turbo lag on acceleration. Boost was set at 7.5psi (although early press releases claimed 8.5psi), and the turbocharger's wastegate was fitted with a tamper-proof seal.

To avoid detonation, Tickford added a bespoke electronic ignition system. This was derived from the ECU then used in the Escort RS1600i, modified by its German manufacturers AFT. The ECU depended on a magnetic sensor on the flywheel and was linked to a second ECU that activated a seventh fuel injector at maximum boost above 3500rpm to ensure adequate fuelling.

The standard Bosch injection system was retained but the injection meter was moved to the right-hand side of the engine

111

bay to make room for the intercooler and the large-diameter charge air pipe leading from it to the plenum on top of the engine. This was a single-piece item made of stainless steel. The battery also had to be moved, and was relocated in the boot. Meanwhile, the air cleaner was moved to the space between inner and outer front right-hand wings, where it received cool air from the intake slot in the front spoiler.

To counter the extra heat generated by the turbocharger, Tickford Capris had an uprated six-row radiator with an electric cooling fan. Heat shields around the exhaust protected the power steering pump and the electrical harness that ran down the inner wing. The fuel filter was relocated on top of the inner wing next to the ignition coil, and there was a 16-row oil cooler behind the front valance.

The standard Capri exhaust was normally retained, but it was possible to order a big-bore stainless steel system at extra cost.

Transmission and rear axle

The Tickford Capri could have either an automatic or a five-speed manual gearbox. For the manual type there were modifications to improve the lubrication of the input shaft and the mainshaft. These changes were later incorporated on standard five-speed gearboxes as well. A standard clutch was used.

Dave Cook Racing converted the axle half-shafts from their standard semi-floating configuration to fully-floating in order to withstand the additional torque from the turbocharged engine. The same company prepared the Tickford Capri's limited-slip differential, which was based on a ZF design and had a 40% locking feature. These special differentials were not fitted to the later cars based on the 2.8 Injection Special, which came with a 25% locking differential as standard. All the Tickford Capris had a finned alloy back plate on the axle casing, intended to keep temperatures down.

The alloy wheels have the same design as those on the contemporary standard 2.8-litre cars, but the centre plate covering the wheel nuts has special Tickford identification.

Suspension

The rear suspension was changed considerably to ensure that the handling was up to the additional power and torque of the turbocharged engine. Sideways movement of the axle was restricted by additional locating arms which braced it to the leaf springs; this arrangement is often described as an A-frame. Early press releases mentioned Polymer spacing bushes on either side of the bushes at the forward ends of these arms to eliminate play, but in practice they were not fitted to production cars.

At the front, the standard MacPherson struts were retained, with Bilstein damper inserts. Again, early press releases promised a feature not fitted to production cars, which was roller-bearing top mounts.

Steering and brakes

The steering was unchanged from the standard 2.8i Capri. Front brakes were the standard ventilated discs but had harder Don 600 pads, and the rear brakes became solid discs with a 10.43in diameter. The rear brake calipers are said to have been based on those used on the Peugeot 504.

Wheels and tyres

The wheels were standard 2.8i or 2.8 Injection Special rims, with a silver finish. There was a special centre cap with the Tickford emblem. All Tickford Capris came with Goodyear NCT low-profile tyres as standard equipment, but Pirelli P7 tyres were a cost option.

Dashboard and interior

Although the basic dashboard and controls were carried over from the host 2.8-litre Capri, Tickford added polished walnut to the instrument panel and the passenger's side of the dashboard, trimmed the facia in grey leather, and added a leather map pocket in front of the glovebox. The very last cars (possibly just two, built in 1987) had Black Ash wood trim in place of the walnut. A Cobra alarm system was part of the standard equipment, and its red tell-tale light was located to the left of the ash tray.

Tickford Capris had a special centre console below the main dashboard, with a matching walnut face-plate and leather trimming. On early cars, this centre console incorporated a Veglia clock, a Lucas boost gauge for the turbocharger, and switches for the standard electric windows. When the optional Electric Pack was specified, switches for the electric mirrors were added above the two dials. On the later cars, from around January 1986, the clock and the boost gauge were relocated where the radio normally sat on the dashboard, and the radio was moved down to the centre console.

Cars based on 2.8i models had standard 2.8i Recaro seats with full cloth upholstery, complemented by door cards, rear quarter panels and steering wheel trimmed in grey

AFTERMARKET SPECIALS

The Tickford cars had a quite distinctively different dash, with figured wood panelling and a leather-trimmed steering wheel that featured the Tickford name on its hub. Clear in these two pictures is the different shift grip for the automatic gearbox. The Tickford console was unique to the cars, and was trimmed in leather. Also visible here is the map pocket in the passenger's footwell. The graphic equaliser for the ICE system that is mounted under the dashboard was not a standard fitting – but very much in period.

A touch of class, perhaps: there were special kick-plates on the sills, visible as soon as a door was opened.

The front seats are branded Recaros, and the upholstery here is the standard half-leather type.

The door trims were also unique on the Tickford cars, with cloth centre panels and velour lower panels. Note the rather crude blanking plug where the window winders would have been on standard cars.

leather to match the dashboard. The steering wheel also had a special triangular boss. Cars based on the 2.8 Injection Special retained that model's half-leather upholstery but no longer had the leather-trimmed door cards and rear quarter panels, or the triangular steering wheel boss. Full leather upholstery was available as an extra-cost option, and the 1984 Motor Show car had an eye-catching interior trimmed in red and white leather, but that appears to have remained unique. On all production cars, carpets were made of a grey

The rear seats have the same split-fold configuration as on other Mk III Capris

The parcels shelf was trimmed to tone in with the interior colours, although it was far from a perfect match.

velour material, but Wilton caret was available at extra cost. A wool headlining was also available as an option.

Boot interior

The relocated battery was mounted on the left-hand side of the boot area and was concealed under a box that was trimmed in grey to match the load area. The wooden false floor of the boot was modified to suit, as was the boot carpet.

IDENTIFICATION

The vehicle identification plates of a Mk II Capri will be found on the bonnet slam panel. The black-printed silver plate is the actual identification plate, and the plate nearer the camera which is painted in the body colour is the Body Plate that was used during the manufacturing process. In this case, it is on an all-black Capri 2.0 S.

MK II CAPRI IDENTIFICATION

The identification plate of a Mk II Capri is attached by rivets to the right-hand side (left when standing in front of the car) of the bonnet slam panel, just inboard of the right-hand headlamp. The chassis number is also stamped into the bodyshell in two other places. It is stamped into the floor between the right-hand front seat and the sill (where it is visible by lifting the carpet), and it is also stamped into the horizontal top surface of the right-hand inner wing

The plate itself is made of metal and is printed in black, leaving unprinted panels into which the relevant details are stamped. The stamping is in relief (ie was done from behind the plate). The whole thing generally resembles the later type used on Mk I Capri models.

Most of the panels also have headings in both English and German, and the plates on British-built and German-built cars are essentially the same. Unsurprisingly, British-built cars have a plate headed "Ford Motor Co Ltd, London England", while the plate on German-built cars is headed "Ford Werke AG Köln, Western Germany."

As on the Mk I identification plates, there are three rows of panels below the headings. The chassis number is in the top row, and decoding the information in the other rows can be very helpful in determining whether a car still has its original build specification.

APPENDIX A: IDENTIFICATION

The top row

The three boxes in the top row are labelled "Typ/Type", "Version", and "Fahrgestell/Vehicle No." The second box is usually left blank; the first box is sometimes blank as well. When it is filled in, it typically has a four-letter code such as BECP. The B indicates a British-built car (G indicates a German-built car); E stands for Capri and the C for two-door (coupé) body. The final P indicates that it is the variant introduced in 1974 (ie a Mk II, although Mk III models used the same identification letter).

The third box in that top row contains the car's 11-character chassis number. These numbers consist of a six-letter prefix followed by a five-digit serial number, which is always between 00001 and 99999. A typical number for a Mk II Capri might be

BBECRD34512.

This decodes as follows:

- B Built in Britain (German-built cars have a G here)
- B Built at Halewood factory
     (C for the German factory in Cologne)
- E Capri
- C Two-door body
- R Calendar year of build
     (note that this is NOT model-year)
- D Month of build

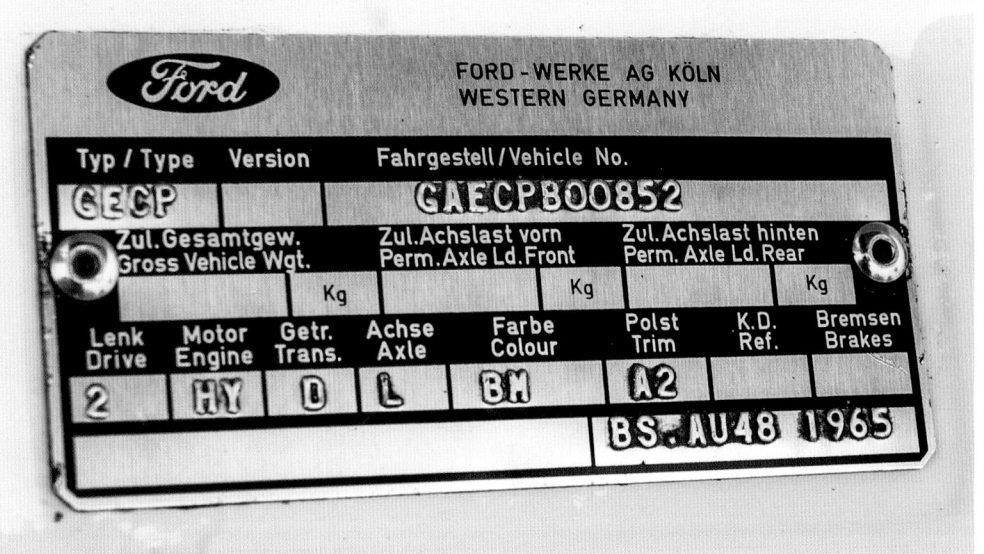

This early plate is on a 1975-model 3-litre Ghia, built before the wholesale changeover to production in Germany but nevertheless showing that this is a car built at the Cologne plant. Note that the safety-belt compliance details (at the bottom right of the plate) are stamped.

Those last two letters can be further decoded, as follows.

Fifth letter

P	1974	S	1976	U	1978
R	1975	T	1977		

Sixth letter
To indicate the month of build, Ford used the same 16-letter sequence as on Mk I Capris.

	Jan	Feb	Mar	Apr	May	Jun	Jly	Aug	Sep	Oct	Nov	Dec
1974	L	Y	S	T	J	U	M	P	B	R	A	G
1975	C	K	D	E	L	Y	S	T	J	U	M	P
1976	B	R	A	G	C	K	D	E	L	Y	S	T
1977	J	U	M	P	B	R	A	G	C	K	D	E
1978	L	Y	S									

FACTORY-ORIGINAL FORD CAPRI MK II & MK III

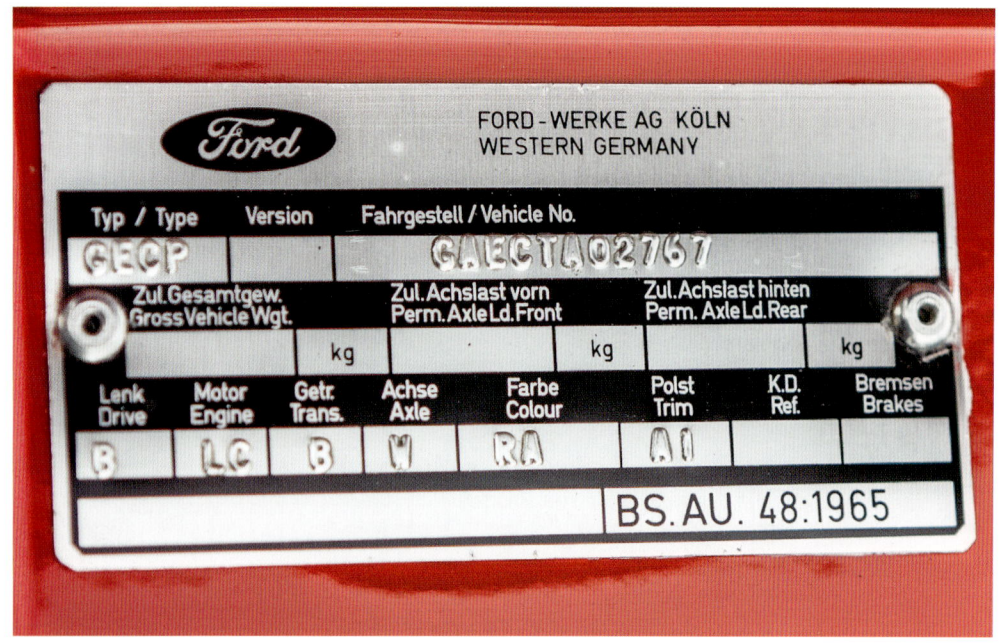

This plate is from 1977, by which time all Capri production was in Germany. In this case, the safety-belt compliance details are printed onto the plate.

The middle row

Moving on to the second row of panels, there are again three boxes, and all of them are typically left blank. They are for "Zul. Gesamtgew/Gross Vehicle Wgt", "Zul. Achslast vorn/Perm. Axle Ld Front" and "Zul. Achslast hinten/Per. Axle Ld Rear", all of which can be recorded in kilograms (kg). UK regulations required no entries here; by contrast, German regulations did require axle loading figures.

The third row

The third row contains eight panels. Working from the left, these begin with the "Lenk/Drive" panel, which will contain a single letter. On Mk II Capris, A stands for RHD and B for LHD.

The second panel is for "Motor/Engine", and this reveals both the nominal size of engine fitted when the car was new and the variant of that engine. The first letter indicates the engine size, as follows:

J	1300	N	2000
L	1600	H	3000.

The second character, which may be a letter or a number, indicates the engine type:

1	OHV (ie Kent) in-line, low compression
2	OHV (ie Kent) in-line, high compression
3	OHV (ie Kent) in-line, GT version
A	OHC (ie Pinto) in-line, low compression
C	OHC (ie Pinto) in-line, high compression
E	OHC (ie Pinto) in-line, GT version
V	V4 or V6, mediumcompression
W	V4 or V6, low compression
X	V4 or V6, low compression
Y	V4 or V6, high compression
Z	V4 or V6, GT version

The third panel is labelled "Getr/Trans", the full words being Getriebe and Transmission. There are just two options here, which are B (or 5) for a four-speed manual gearbox and D (or 7) for a three-speed automatic.

Next comes "Achse/Axle", which reveals the final drive ratio. The options are:

B	3.75:1
C	3.89:1
L	3.09:1
N	4.11:1
R	3.22:1
S	3.44:1
W	3.77:1
X	4.125:1
Z	3.54:1

APPENDIX A: IDENTIFICATION

The fifth panel is for "Farbe/Colour" and the sixth is for "Polst/Trim". Finally, there is a panel labelled KD Ref – relevant only to overseas assembly operations and not used for UK-market Mk II Capris – and one labelled "Bremsen/Brakes" which is normally blank (although cars sold in Italy had a digit here to meet local requirements).

The identification number of a Capri Mk II was also stamped into the body before it was painted. The number is preceded and followed by an additional indentation, and is located on the horizontal top surface of the right-hand inner front wing.

It is in fact quite rare to find a Capri's identification plate in anything like good condition. Most have worn over the years and are likely to look like this one, which is on the 3.0-litre John Player Special car.

Incontrovertible proof that a car is what it claims to be: this is the body plate on a John Player Special model.

FACTORY-ORIGINAL FORD CAPRI MK II & MK III

CAPRI MK III IDENTIFICATION

The identification plate of a Mk III Capri is attached by rivets to the right-hand side (left when standing in front of the car) of the bonnet slam panel, just inboard of the right-hand headlamp. The chassis number is also stamped into the bodyshell in two other places. It is stamped into the floor between the right-hand front seat and the sill (where it is visible by lifting the carpet), and it is also stamped into the metal on top of the right-hand inner wing.

There were two types of identification plate on Mk III Capris, and the changeover coincided with Ford's change from its own chassis numbers to standardised VIN identification. The earlier type of plate is the same as the type seen on late Mk II models, and was used up to the end of 1980. The VIN type of plate that was used from January 1981 has far less printing on it. In fact, at first glance these later plates appear to have almost no printing – which can often be the case on an old and worn plate. Both types of plate are made of very thin aluminium and are screen-printed in black, leaving unprinted panels into which the relevant details are stamped. The stamping is in relief (ie was done from behind the plate).

1978-1980 plates

These plates have the Ford symbol at top left, and next to in is "Ford-Werke Aktiengesellschaft" (Ford works, stock company). Although this heading is in German, most of the panels on the main section of the plate have headings in both English and French.

There are two vertical rows of panels, with an additional row of four panels at the bottom. The chassis number is in the second column of the right-hand row, but decoding the information in the other rows can be very helpful in determining whether a car still has its original build specification. Note that from 1981, the Ford chassis number gave way to a VIN (Vehicle Identification Number) that conformed to new internationally agreed standards.

The left-hand column

The two boxes above the left-hand fixing rivet are labelled "Drive/Cond" (Cond for Conduite) and "Engine/Motor" (although the correct French word is actually Moteur). In the first box, 1 stands for LHD and 2 for RHD – so all UK-market cars will have a 2 here. In the second box, the letters will be from the following list:

HY	3.0-litre Essex V6
J2	1.3-litre Kent, high-compression
LE	1.6-litre Pinto
LC	1.6-litre "GT" Pinto (ie 1.6 S)
NE	2.0-litre Pinto

The configuration of the VIN-type identity plate, seen here on a Mk III Ghia, is quite different from those seen on Mk II models.

This is the build plate on that Mk III Ghia – full of useful information that cannot at present be decoded.

APPENDIX A: IDENTIFICATION

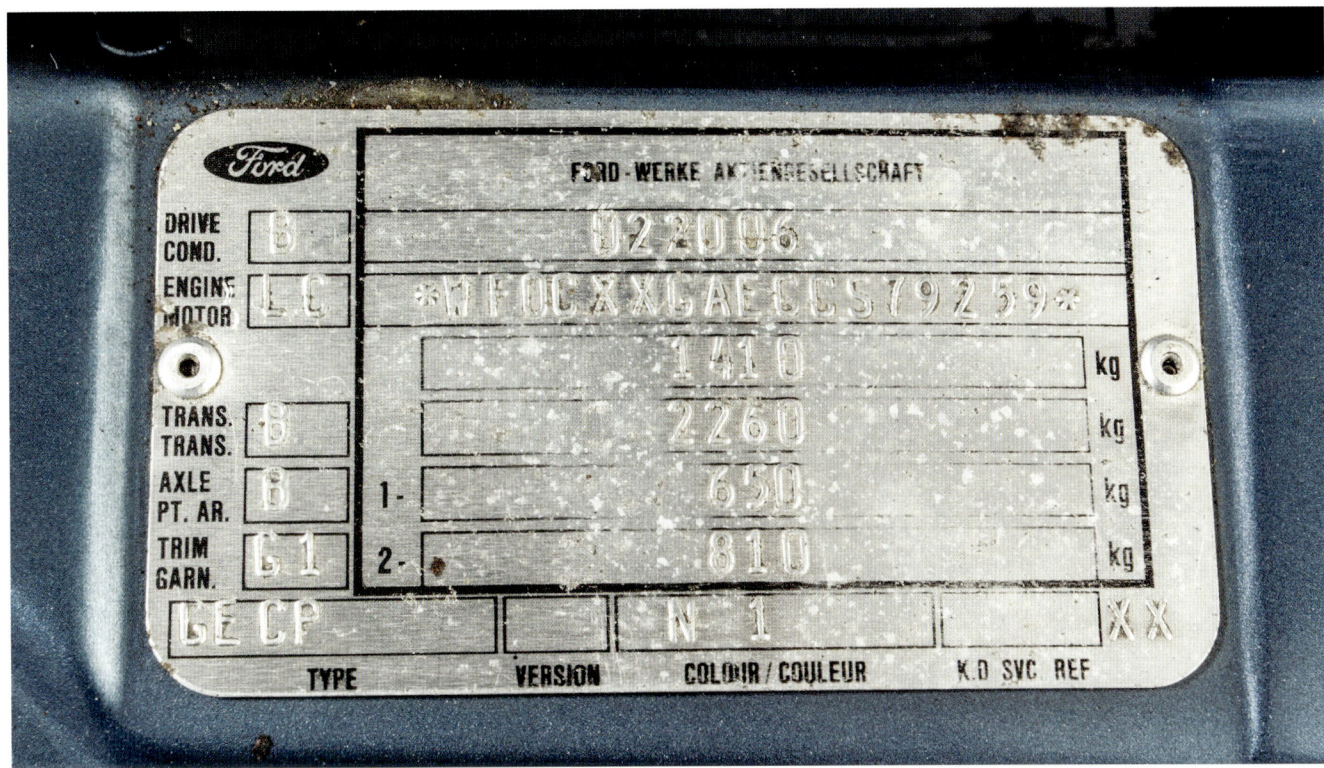

The identity plate on this Mk III Calypso has the same configuration as the one on the earlier Ghia, but the boxes are labelled in English and French rather than in German and Spanish. The build plate's meaning is once again tantalisingly out of reach.

Below the fixing rivet, the three boxes are labelled "Trans/Trans" (Transmission), "Axle/Pt Ar" (Pont Arrière, or Rear Axle), and "Trim/Gar" (Garniture). The transmission type will be B for a four-speed manual or D for an automatic; the list of axle options is shown below; and there will be a pair of Trim letters.

The options in the "Axle" box are:

B   3.75:1
L   3.09:1
S   3.44:1
W   3.77:1
X   4.125:1

The right-hand column

The two top panels in the second column have no identifying legend. The top one carries a number and letter code such as 204T. The second panel has the chassis number or VIN, both of which are explained below. Below this are four boxes containing weights, and each one has the letters "kg" (kilogrammes) printed to its right. The top box is the car's Unladen Weight in kilogrammes (eg 1410); below it is the maximum laden weight (eg 2260); the third box is the maximum weight permitted over the front axle (eg 650) and the last one is the maximum weight permitted over the rear axle (eg 810).

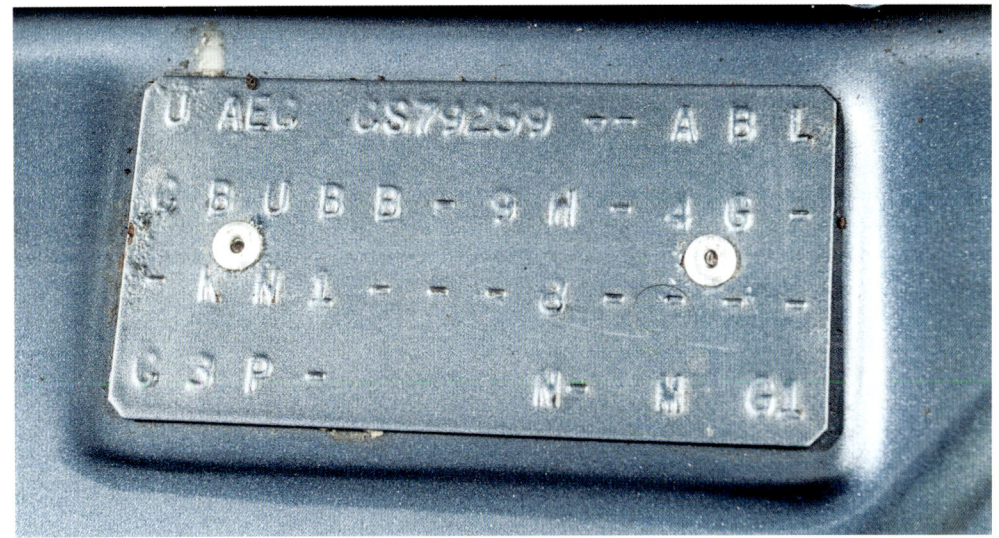

The bottom row

The bottom four boxes, reading from left to right, are labelled Type, Version, Colour/Couleur and KD Sync Ref. The Type box might be stamped SECP (Saarlouis, Capri, Two-door body, 1974 variant – note that Mk IIs also used the P code).

The second panel is often left blank but the third panel will contain a colour code. The fourth panel is not relevant to UK-market cars, as all were delivered in fully-built condition.

121

FORD CHASSIS NUMBERS

On Capris built before the end of 1980, the second panel in the right-hand column contains the car's 12-character chassis number. These numbers consist of a six-letter prefix followed by a six-digit serial number, which is always between 10001 and 99999. They are always preceded and followed by an asterisk (to meet legal requirements).

A typical number for a Mk III Capri might be

GCECAG451230.

This decodes as follows:

G	Built by Ford Germany
C	Built at Cologne factory (S for the Saarlouis factory)
E	Capri
C	Two-door body
A	Calendar year of build (note that this is NOT model-year)
G	Month of build

Those last two letters can be further decoded, as follows.

Fifth letter

U	1978	B	1981	E	1984
W	1979	C	1982	F	1985
A	1980	D	1983	G	1986

Sixth letter

To indicate the month of build, Ford used the same 16-letter sequence as on earlier Capris.

	Jan	Feb	Mar	Apr	May	Jun	Jly	Aug	Sep	Oct	Nov	Dec
1978		S	T	J	U	M	P	B	R	A	G	
1979	C	K	D	E	L	Y	S	T	J	U	M	P
1980	B	R	A	G	C	K	D	E	L	Y	S	T
1981	J	U	M	P	B	R	A	G	C	K	D	E
1982	L	Y	S	T	J	U	M	P	B	R	A	G
1983	C	K	D	E	L	Y	S	T	J	U	M	P
1984	B	R	A	G	C	K	D	E	L	Y	S	T
1985	J	U	M	P	B	R	A	G	C	K	D	E
1986	L	Y	S	T	J	U	M	P	B	R	A	G

APPENDIX A: IDENTIFICATION

1981-1986 PLATES

The VIN-type plates have a different configuration, with the Ford oval at top left and "Ford-Werke-Aktiengesellschaft" above the right-hand set of columns.

There are five small boxes in the left-hand column. On some plates these are labelled in German and Spanish, and on others they are in English and French. Reading from the top, they are as follows:

German and Spanish	English and French	Meaning
Lenk/Cond	Drive/Cond	Steering position
Motor/Motor	Engine/Motor	Engine type
Getr/Trans	Trans/Trans	Gearbox type
Achse/Eje	Axle /Pt Ar	Rear axle type
Polst/Tapic	Trim/Garn	Upholstery type

There are six larger panels in the right-hand column. The top one contains a build code and the second one contains the VIN. Below that are four boxes, each one labelled "kg" on the right, and the bottom two labelled "1-" and "2-" on the left. These show weights.

Across the bottom of the plate are four more boxes, with labels as follows:

German and Spanish	English and French	Meaning
Tpp/Tipo	Type	Type (ie Capri)
Version	Version	Version (ie Model)
Farbe/Couleur	Colour/Couleur	Colour
KD SVC Ref	KD SVC Ref	(For CKD only)

Note that "Tpp" on the German and Spanish version is actually a misprint for "Typ". The space for KD kit details was not used on cars sold in Britain, which were obviously imported in fully built form.

VIN DECODING

The VIN codes used from January 1981 depended on a completely different system, with 17-character identifiers consisting of a 12-digit prefix code followed by a five-digit serial number. A typical VIN on a Mk III Capri might be WFOCXXGAECEA29103, which looks like a meaningless string of letters and numbers until it is broken down. It breaks down like this:

WFO	Ford (world manufacturer code)
C	Two-door coupé (body type)
XX	Check digits (may be letters or numbers, to prevent fraud)
G	Ford Germany (branch responsible)
A	Build factory (A = Saarlouis, G = Cologne)
E	Capri (body type)
C	Capri (model)
E	Year (see separate table)
A	Month (see separate table)
29103	Five-digit sequential number.

The last-of-line Capri has been preserved by Ford in the UK, and has VIN WFOCXXGAECGG11896. Note the A code suggesting Saarlouis build!

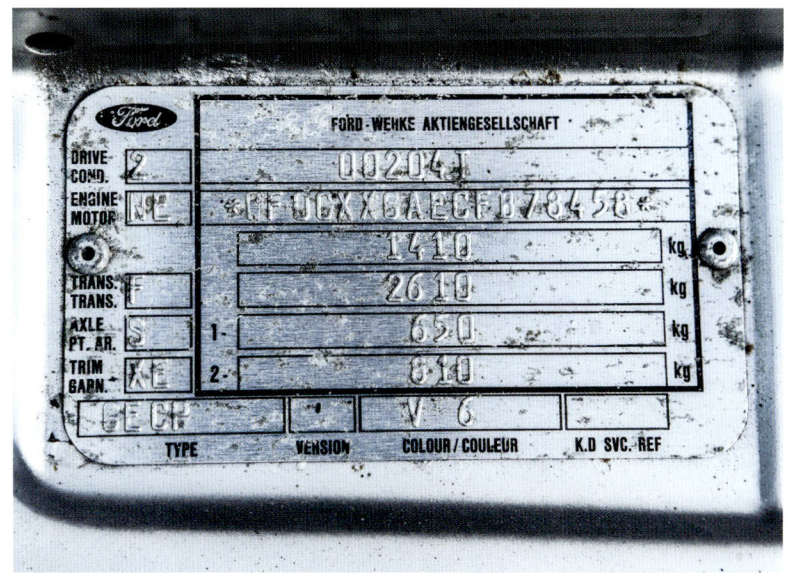

The 1985 Laser has its build plate in English and French again, while the build plate again awaits further research before it will yield its secrets.

GLASS DATING

This is typical of the markings on Sekurit glass, and is seen on a 1985 Mk III Laser model. The figure 5 clearly indicates 1985 manufacture, and the single dot before it indicates the month of January.

The companies that supplied glass for the Mk II and Mk III Capris marked their products with a series of identification codes, and these codes include a date of manufacture.

This code system makes it possible to determine whether the glass on a particular car is likely to be original to it or not. However, it is not an infallible guide to the date of the car's manufacture, and glass would typically have been made just before the car was assembled. Variations of one month either way in glass sets should not be taken as incontrovertible proof that some glass has been replaced.

Triplex glass

The glass on Halewood-built Capris was made by Triplex and its approximate date of manufacture can be determined from dots etched into the glass above or below the words "Triplex" and "Toughened" (or "Laminated" when appropriate).

The quarter was indicated by a dot above one of four letters in the Triplex name, as follows:

T	R	E	X
First quarter	Second quarter	Third quarter	Fourth quarter
(Jan-Mar)	(Apr-June)	(July-Sept)	(Oct-Dec).

The dots below the letters decode the year, as follows

T	O	U	G	H	E	N	E	D
1	2	3	4	5	6	7	8	9

L	A	M	I	N	A	T	E	D
1	2	3	4	5	6	7	8	9

Note that the decade of manufacture is not revealed by these codes, although in the case of a Mk II Capri it is in any case likely to be obvious.

So a dot above the X of Triplex and one below the H of Toughened would indicate glass manufactured between October and December 1975.

When no dot is present, the figure represented is a 0. In some cases, the 0 seems to have been represented by a dot under the space following the last letter.

Sekurit glass

The German-built cars mostly have glass supplied by Sekurit, which uses a far simpler date-coding system. This is usually located at the bottom of the group of glass information, and consists of a single number with dots either before it or after it.

The single number shows the year within a particular decade. The figure 5 on a Capri Mk III would therefore indicate 1985. Dots before this figure indicate a month of manufacture in the first half of the year; so, two dots indicate the second month (February), and six dots the sixth month (June). Dots after the figure indicate a month of manufacture in the second half of the year; so, three dots indicate the ninth month (September), and five dots indicate the eleventh month (November).